The Political Economy of
Development in India

Extracts from Reviews

'... the paradigm of dominant propertied classes provides an alternative view of India to that offered by the new political economy... What it attempts to do is no less than to integrate both the analysis of rent-seeking and the analysis of urban bias into a more comprehensive overall framework of ideas... Bardhan is a skilled exponent of this ambitious scheme. His work is certainly a minor masterpiece of compression, which is achieved at little cost in either clarity of outline, or richness of detail.'

—John Toye, *Modern Asian Studies*

'I can only compliment Pranab Bardhan, not just on his well-known competence as an economist, but on his courage in taking major risks in a broader analysis. Most of the recent efforts to write a political economy of India have been undertaken by political scientists and journalists; it is good to have an economist make such an attempt.'

—George Rosen, *Economic Development and Cultural Change*

'While the book relates a grim story, he does not preclude the possibility that Indian society will discover creative ways of meshing democratic processes with the requirements of economic growth. He has performed a notable service in making so clear the importance and magnitude of that challenge.'

—Karl de Schweinitz, *Journal of Economic Issues*

The Political Economy of Development in India

Expanded edition with an epilogue on the
political economy of reform in India

PRANAB BARDHAN

OXFORD
UNIVERSITY PRESS

OXFORD
UNIVERSITY PRESS

YMCA Library Building, Jai Singh Road, New Delhi 110001

Oxford University Press is a department of the University of Oxford. It furthers
the University's objective of excellence in research, scholarship, and education
by publishing worldwide in

Oxford   New York

Auckland   Cape Town   Dar es Salaam   Hong Kong   Karachi
Kuala Lumpur   Madrid   Melbourne   Mexico City   Nairobi
New Delhi   Shanghai   Taipei   Toronto

With offices in

Argentina   Austria   Brazil   Chile   Czech Republic   France   Greece
Guatemala   Hungary   Italy   Japan   Poland   Portugal   Singapore
South Korea   Switzerland   Thailand   Turkey   Ukraine   Vietnam

Oxford is a registered trade mark of Oxford University Press
in the UK and in certain other countries

Published in India
by Oxford University Press, New Delhi

The moral rights of the author have been asserted
Database right Oxford University Press (maker)
First published in 1984 by Basil Blackwell Publisher Ltd.,
108 Cowley Road, Oxford, UK
First Indian impression 1985
Published by arrangement with the original publisher
Oxford India Paperbacks 1989
Expanded edition 1998
Eighth impression 2008

ISBN-13: 978-0-19-564770-9
ISBN-10: 0-19-564770-X

Printed at Wadhwa International, New Delhi 110 020
Published by Oxford University Press
YMCA Library Building, Jai Singh Road, New Delhi 110 001

Contents

Preface

This book is an expanded version of the 1982–83 Radhakrish-
nan Memorial Lectures that I delivered at All Souls College,
Oxford. The format of public lectures often provides the
freedom to make sweeping surveys, indulge in wanton
generalizations, venture into polemical speculations   in
general to let the world in on the bees in one's bonnet without
the dull obligations of a monograph to follow up the breezy
observations with lengthy qualifications, ponderous footnotes
and technical appendices. I have used the freedom quite
liberally, taking on the vast panorama of the political economy
of development in contemporary India in a few quick,
impetuous brush-strokes. In the subsequent pages the reader
will, therefore, find much that is controversial, opinionated
and (I hope) provocative. I have tried to discern some patterns
in the chaotic and seemingly disconnected events in the
political and economic life of India in recent years, not all
of which easily lend themselves to such schematic interpreta-
tions. The running theme of the book involves a number of
oversimplified hypotheses which, given the nature of complex decision-making processes in the polity and their impact
on the economy, are often difficult to test with quantifiable
data, although in the process of my examination of those
hypotheses I have tried to press into service as much 'hard'
statistical evidence as the general format of this book will
allow. While as a professional economist I am trained to feel

somewhat uncomfortable in this slippery terrain of no easy quantifiability, particularly on questions involving political judgment, I have found the issues challenging and rewarding in ways which no practitioner of economics dealing only with 'solved political problems' (to use Abba Lerner's phrase) can experience.

Much of my earlier research on the Indian economy has been concerned with studying different aspects of poverty, measurement of its trends, its socio-economic characterization and the institutional mechanisms of its perpetuation or reproduction. In this book, however, not merely do I step away from my micro-studies to get an overview, but my main focus is on some of the political processes governing accumulation, rather than distribution. My concern here is particularly with the political economy of the constraints that seem to have blocked the economy's escape from a low-level equilibrium trap of slow growth, which is more of an analytical puzzle than the question of why the poor in India do not get a better deal. I have also tried in general to resist the twin temptations of prescription (of what is to be done) and prognostication (about what is going to happen); my major objective here is to understand what has happened.

On the first draft of the manuscript I have received very useful comments from Mrinal Datta Choudhuri, Ashok Desai, Michael Lipton, Ashok Rudra, Amartya Sen, T.N. Srinivasan, A. Vaidyanathan and participants of a workshop around that draft organized by the Joint Committee on South Asia of the Social Science Research Council and the American Council of Learned Societies at Cambridge, Massachusetts in October 1983. Since many of these friends have a substantially different view from mine on some of the issues discussed, I would like to take this opportunity to absolve them of all guilt by association.

P.B.
February 1984

1

Introduction

I am told that mothers in the affluent western countries often urge their children to finish their plates by reminding them of the hungry people of India. It may or may not be an effective strategy to make the rich eat more in the name of the poor, but it is interesting to recall that only a few centuries back the children in some of those same countries grew up with stories of the fabulous riches of India; some of them as adults ventured out to find the quickest routes to India, even stumbling on new continents on the way. But over the last century or two India has been more often associated with endemic hunger or poverty, and the stories of the extravagant wealth and splendour of the Maharajas have not succeeded in dispelling that association. At the time of her Independence in 1947, following several decades of economic stagnation (if not decay) under British rule, India was one of the poorest countries in the world. It was the great hope and aspiration of the founding fathers of the Indian republic to relieve this crushing burden of poverty. Over the years, five-year plan documents, political speeches and electoral slogans have reiterated this primary goal in endless litany, yet, after more than three decades, India remains one of the poorest countries of the world, in fact probably the largest single-country contributor to the pool of the world's poor.

Introduction

There has been extensive discussion in India on the question of the measurement of poverty. If one takes Rs 15 per caput per month at 1960–61 prices as a rough 'poverty line' in rural areas,[1] and if one uses the agricultural labour consumer price index to approximate the price rise faced by the rural poor, then on the basis of household consumer expenditure data, like those in Table 1, collected by the National Sample Survey (NSS) one can say that in 1977–78 about 40 per cent of the rural population was below this poverty line.[2] Similarly, if one takes Rs 20 per caput per month at 1960 prices as the urban poverty line (the urban cost of living being higher than the rural), and if one uses the industrial worker consumer price index to approximate the price rise faced by the urban poor, one can estimate from NSS data that in 1977–78 about 39 per cent of the urban population was below this poverty line. By this count the numbers of people below the poverty line in India today exceed the *total* population of the Soviet Union, the third largest country of the world. Of course, such rough and ready estimates of people in poverty leave a lot of scope for improvement, both in the methods of measurement and in

[1] This is the poverty line that has been used in Bardhan (1970, 1973), Dandekar and Rath (1971), Ahluwalia, M.S. (1978), and others. Sukhatme (1978) has pointed to the problems of assuming average nutritional norms on account of the interpersonal variability of nutritional needs and the existence of adaptive mechanisms in the human body. The NSS household consumption estimates used in the literature are in any case not very appropriate in measuring *undernutrition*; the poverty estimates should more appropriately be interpreted as a rough measure of income (or expenditure) inadequacy in buying a given consumption basket.

[2] The tables have all been collected together in an Appendix at the end of the book, see pp. 87–109. The estimates above are, of course, body-count estimates of the poor, giving equal weight to someone who is extremely poor and someone who is just below the poverty line. The Sen (1974) index of poverty, which takes this into account, turns out to be 0.14 for rural India in 1977–78. In general, the *time-pattern* of the body-count estimates and Sen indices of poverty has been quite similar in rural India in the last two decades.

2

the data base,[3] but there is no doubt that by any account the numbers will be staggering.[4]

If one moves away from figures of poverty derived from consumer expenditure data and looks at indicators of some of the elemental aspects of life, the picture is equally grim. The infant mortality rate in 1981 was 121 per thousand (more than one and a half times that of China). In 1978 the death rate for children of up to 4 years of age was 45 for males and 52 for females (with the average, as well as the male–female differential, much higher in some States like Uttar Pradesh, as Table 3 indicates). In 1976 more than three-quarters of all live births in rural India did not have the benefit of access to any trained medical practitioners. Two-thirds of the total population of India do not have access to safe drinking water. About half of the villages do not have a road or a single electricity connection. Nearly one-third of primary-school-age children is not enrolled in school (in contrast to less than 10 per cent in China) and nearly two-thirds of the adult population (in contrast to one-third in China) are illiterate (female literacy lagging far behind male).

Over the last decades the Government has launched several programmes aimed at tackling directly the problems of poverty, unemployment, disease and illiteracy. Some of them have been reasonably successful in localized regions: for instance, the Employment Guarantee Scheme at a minimum rural wage in the State of Maharashtra; the *Antyodaya* scheme in the State of Rajasthan which aimed at uplifting

[3] For a discussion of these problems, see Bardhan and Srinivasan (1974).

[4] Many of these poor people are not unemployed. The NSS Employment and Unemployment Survey data, as in Table 2, suggest that the unemployment rate was 7.7 per cent in rural areas and 10.3 per cent in urban areas in 1977–78. In a country where the government in general does not provide unemployment benefits, many of the poor cannot afford to remain unemployed for long. Low and unstable income per earner and a low earner-dependent ratio in the family are more commonly associated with poverty than unemployment. Yet, as Table 2 makes clear, the unemployment rate is much above average for the poor.

the poorest of the poor by helping them to acquire income-earning assets; the preferential loans which, under the Small Farmer Development Agency programmes, successfully reached some farmers with holdings of less than two hectares in many districts and so on. There has also been some general progress over the years in the provision of public consumption and welfare measures for the poor in the form of health and sanitation, drinking water, nutrition, housing, education, transport, roads, communication and electricity. But the facilities created remain woefully meagre in proportion to the total minimum needs, even though the funds earmarked for such programmes constitute a significant fraction of the Government budget every year. Apart from the actue problems of developing an adequte administrative delivery infrastructure in the widely scattered and remote regions of poverty, and of coming to terms with the associated managerial and organizational bottlenecks,[5] finance has been a major constraint. Whenever there is a general financial squeeze, which is much too often, the axe usually falls most heavily on the social welfare programmes for the poor. It is also well known that there are considerable 'leakages' of funds and benefits from these programmes, partly from the delivery pipeline itself (enriching middlemen, contractors, corrupt officials, etc.) and partly from the diversion of benefits at the end of the pipeline in favour of upper-income, non-target recipients (for example, in cases of low-cost housing, education, transport and communication facilities, subsidized co-operative credit, etc.). That the Government can easily get away with the budget cuts on these programmes, and that the middlemen and the non-target groups can get away with the leakages is, of course, largely a measure of the political weakness of the intended beneficiaries – the poor –

---

[5] In many cases, the lack of co-ordinated, well-designed, decentralized schemes at the local level has led to non-utilization or misutilization of funds even when finance is available. For some examples, see Dantawala (1983).

as an organized interest group. The small farmers and agricultural laborers, artisans and the self-employed in household enterprises, petty traders and casual non-agricultural workers constitute the bulk of the poor. Organized group actions on their part, or agitations for their basic social and economic rights, are still highly fragmentary, localized and infrequent.

Of course, apart from direct welfare measures, the process of economic growth itself can benefit the poor, even though the rich appropriate a disproportionate share. In India there have been never-ending debates on whether the benefits of economic growth 'trickle down' to the poor or not. It is clear from cross-section evidence[6] that by and large areas of sustained high growth (like Punjab and Haryana) are also areas where the percentage of population below the poverty line is the lowest. But the limited NSS *time-series* data at the State level do not yield clear-cut evidence: for example, in States with high agricultural growth (like Punjab, Haryana and Gujarat) there has been no trend decline in the percentage of rural population below the poverty line over the last two decades, nor is there much of a statistically significant relationship between the extent of rural poverty and the volume of agricultural production per head of rural population in these States.[7] While agricultural growth obviously generates forces that tend to improve the incomes of small farmers and wage labourers, in some institutional environments it may also unleash forces that may partially counteract the positive effects for the poor, through: (a) the adoption of labour-displacing machinery; (b) the increased profitability of self-cultivation by large farmers, leading to eviction of small tenants; (c) the increased dependence of agriculture on

---

[6] In a linear regression analysis of cross-section evidence from 56 agro-climatic NSS regions, we found that the percentage of rural population below the poverty line in a region in 1972–73 is negatively and significantly related to the average annual rate of growth of crop output in that region. See Bardhan (1983).

[7] See Ahluwalia, M.S. (1984).

purchased inputs and privately controlled irrigation, driving some small farmers, with limited access to resources and credit, out of cultivation and into crowding the wage-labour market; (d) a similar crowding of the wage-labour market by displaced village artisans, as the demand pattern of the new rural rich shifts away from local handicrafts and services towards mass-produced urban consumer goods and services, and so on. In the non-agricultural sector, the possible negative forces of growth for the poor involve a similar displacement caused by capital-intensive industrialization and lop-sided urbanization, while in the countryside expansion of the mining and timber industries leads to decimation of forests and the economic basis of tribal life. This is a familiar story in many parts of the world. But in most of India, while these uprooting and dispossessing effects of economic growth are not absent or unimportant, the persistence of mass poverty may have at least as much to do with the sluggishness of growth itself. There simply hasn't been enough growth for its benefits to trickle down. Over the last thirty years or so (between 1950–51 and 1981–82), the trend rate of economic growth has been fairly constant at the low rate of about 3.5 per cent per year, although annual fluctuations around this trend are large. With a population growth rate that does not yet show much sign of deceleration, per caput income over this period has crawled at the constant rate of about 1.4 per cent. At this rate, even if the inequality in the distribution of income remains unchanged, it will be an unconscionably long time before any significant dent is made in the backlog of extreme poverty.

Inequality of income is quite high in India: on the basis of data collected by the National Council of Applied Economic Research it has been estimated that in the mid-seventies the top quintile of households enjoyed about half of the total disposable household income, while the bottom quintile had a share of only 7 per cent. By all accounts the distribution of assets (physical and, particularly, human capital) is much more unequal. It should also be added that compared to many other societies the same inequality is more oppressive on the poor in India not merely because of the absolute rock-bottom average level of living, but also on account of the *social* degradation that afflicts the life of many of the under-privileged groups.

International comparability of income distribution data is notoriously difficult, but, for whatever it is worth, it may be noted, on the basis of estimates for selected developing countries put together by the World Bank (see Table 4), that household income inequality in India is *less* than in many other semi-industrial developing countries like Brazil, Mexico, Turkey, Kenya, Thailand, and the Philippines (the Indian household income distribution seems to 'Lorenz-dominate'[8] that of any of these countries); but it is *greater* than in other semi-industrial countries like Taiwan and Yugoslavia. (The comparison with South Korea is ambiguous: India's distribution of income is less unequal for the bottom 40 per cent, but then for the other quintiles of households the Lorenz curve is more favourable for South Korea.) But it is in the rate of economic growth that *all* of these nine countries dominate India's performance: over the last two decades their rate of growth of income per caput has been at least twice that of India and in some cases even four to five times (note that none of these is an oil-exporting country).

It is, of course, true that the population of all these nine countries taken together is less than two-thirds of the total population of India. In a large country like India, the high growth rates in some regions (which by themselves contain a population size larger than that of many countries: for

---

[8] A country is said to 'Lorenz-dominate' another country in terms of equality of income distribution if, compared to the latter country, the former has at least as high an income share for each cumulative fractile of the poorest population and a strictly higher share for some fractile of the poorest population.

example, the high-growth region of Punjab, Haryana and Delhi taken together has a population larger than that of Kenya, Taiwan or Yugoslavia and about the size of that of South Korea) get diluted by the lower growth in other regions. But even compared to a very large country like China, the Indian per caput income growth has been much slower, actually less than half the Chinese rate over the last two decades on the basis of reported official statistics (again, barring questions of comparability of data).[9]

What are the factors that constrain the growth performance in India? When it comes to reduction of economic inequalities, the standard explanation of unsatisfactory performance often runs in terms of the political clout that the rich have in resisting encroachments on their vested interests. But rapid economic growth should be consistent with the objective of self-aggrandizement of most sections of the Indian rich today. Yet what prevents them from managing its collective achievement? Liberal economists point the accusing finger at the stifling bureaucratic regulations and the economic inefficiencies they spawn. Radical economists emphasize the inherent weaknesses of dependent capitalism in the periphery' of a global accumulation process, and the limitations on the size of domestic effective demand for industrial goods that mass poverty entails. Many public commentators, of course, go beyond all this and bemoan the loss of 'character', decline in 'values', absence of 'work ethic', and the pervading stench of corruption.

---

[9] By most accounts, the income distribution in China is more egalitarian than in India, particularly in the urban sector. Comparing the estimates given by the World Bank (1983a) for China at the end of the seventies and those given by the National Council of Applied Economic Research for India in mid-seventies, the poorest 40 per cent of the population gets about 20 per cent of income in both rural China and India, and 30 per cent of income in urban China and 17 per cent in urban India; the richest 20 per cent of the population gets 39 per cent of income in rural China, 42 per cent in rural India, 28 per cent of income in urban China and 49 per cent in urban India.

In this book I shall not in general discuss questions of social psyche or national character or value systems. I may only note in passing that some of the lamented lapses in values or the propensity of people to corruption are not strikingly different in India from some of the high-growth developing countries we have referred to (or even compared to the history of today's developed countries). History is also replete with instances of values or ethical norms (Protestant or Confucian or Jain) adapting themselves remarkably to changing economic opportunities and trends. In the subsequent pages I shall focus primarily on the political and economic constraints, and bring out the role of public investment in the agricultural and industrial infrastructure, and of public managment of capital, as key determinants of economic growth. In connection with this role of the public sector, I shall explore the nature of the Indian state and its relationship with society, and the kind of economic classes that dominate the latter and the types of pressures for patronage and subsidies that they generate. I shall then try to trace the impact of these forces on the functioning of the economy, especially its growth process, and on the functioning of the polity, especially its democratic process.

2

Growth in Agriculture

It is useful to start by recounting the remarkably favourable preconditions of high economic growth that India possesses in contrast to many other developing countries: a well-diversified resource base, a large domestic market, a reasonably stable political system, a relatively successful experience of national integration (in spite of current troubles in the north-east and the north-west), an experienced bureaucracy, a large fund of entrepreneurial talent, the world's fourth largest pool of scientific and technical manpower (even though it only reflects an aspect of extreme inequality if one keeps in mind that India also happens to be the largest single-country contributor to the world's pool of illiterate people), a fairly elaborate industrial infrastructure, and in recent years a high savings rate and a large inflow of foreign exchange through remittances by Indian migrants abroad. Yet, as we have already noted, over the last three decades per caput income has grown at a very low rate (at less than half the corresponding growth rate of the developing countries of the world taken together).

Let us now look at the sectoral components of this overall growth. Agriculture is, of course, quantitatively the most important sector, contributing more than half of net domestic product (at constant prices) in the early fifties, this proportion having declined to about 40 per cent in the early eighties (as may be checked from Table 5). Value added in agriculture grew at the annual rate of 2.4 per cent in the period of 1950–51 to 1964–65, roughly the first half of the three decades under consideration. In the second half of the period, between 1967–68 and 1981–82 (excluding the abnormally bad crop-years of 1965–66 and 1966–67), it grew at the rate of 2.2 per cent per year. But the difference in the estimated growth rates of the two periods is not statistically significant. Thus the so-called green revolution which is associated with the second period, while it has indeed dramatically improved yields in particular crops (e.g. wheat) in particular regions (e.g. the north-west), has not led to any acceleration in the overall rate of growth in agriculture. Put another way, the yield growth of recent years has barely managed to compensate for the area expansion of earlier years in overall contribution to growth. There has actually been a significant deceleration in the growth of production of commerical crops (oil seeds, fibres, etc.) in the second period, and within foodgrains the production of pulses, a major source of protein for the poor, has been largely stagnant (see Table 6).

There was a substantial expansion in the use of chemical fertilizers and irrigated acreage. Nutrients used per unit of cropped area increased from less than 1 kg. per hectare in the mid-fifties to about 5 kg. in the mid-sixties and to 32 kg. at the beginning of the 1980s. The irrigated proportion of cropped area increased from 17 per cent in the early 1950s, to 20 per cent in the mid-sixties, and to about 31 per cent at the beginning of the 1980s. But these levels of fertilizer use and irrigation are much below those in some other developing countries, for example those is East Asia (including China), and far below their potential levels even in India. A district-wise stuay[1] by the Planning Commission indicated that less than one-fifth of the districts was under improved agricultural

[1] See Planning Commission (1977, p. 48).

practices in terms of the provision of irrigation, high-yielding varieties of seeds, and fertilizer applications. Other studies[2] have shown that traditional yields of major cereals on rain-fed lands which stagnate at 0.7 to 0.8 tonnes per hectare, can be mutliplied 2.5 to 3 times with simultaneous use of these practices. There has been a remarkable increase in private investment in farm assets like irrigation pumps and tractors. Pump-sets, in particular, have increased for farmers who can afford them (or raise the requisite credit) their individual control over water supply which is crucial for agriculture. Yet the latest estimates[3] suggest that about 70 per cent of India's groundwater potential is till unutilized (particularly in North India). There is also some evidence[4] of a recent slowdown in the growth of private investment in agriculture: as a proportion of total investment in physical assets within the household sector, it went on increasing from the early fifties until it reached a peak of about 36 per cent in the mid-sixties, and since then (up to the end of the seventies) it has remained below that level. But even without a slow-down in the growth of private investment, the growth prospects of Indian agriculture will remain vitally dependent on the role of public investment[5] in irrigation, drainage and flood control,[6] in land shaping and land consolidation, in

[2] See, for example, Sarma and Roy (1979).

[3] These revised estimates are based on State-level surveys and recalculations by State Groundwater Organizations on the basis of some new norms. These estimates are, however, quite arbitrary and are subject to large margins of error.

[4] For some of this evidence, see Report of the Working Group on Savings (1982, p. 17). One should, of course, keep in mind that in view of the way household investment in physical assets is computed, the estimates may be somewhat shaky.

[5] Krishnamurthy and Saibaba (1983) estimate that the elasticity of private gross real investment in agriculture with respect to public gross investment in that sector is 0.6.

[6] A recent Public Accounts Committee in the Parliament estimated that in the three decades since 1951 about Rs 150 billion have been spent on irrigation development resulting in a creation of 39 million hectares of irrigation potential, against the target of about 60 million hectares. To cover this shortfall of about 21

12

prevention of soil erosion and salinity, in the development of a widespread research and extension network, and in rural electrification and provision of production credit. All these programmes in agriculture involve externalities and indivisibilities in a large enough way to make the role of the state (and community organizations) absolutely indispensable in the growth process of what is otherwise a privately owned sector.

There has been in India long, and often strident, discussion on the institutional constraints on agricultural growth, particularly on the spread of the green revolution from its north-western sanctuary to the rest of the country. In parts of eastern, central and southern India, the historical legacy of subinfeudation, of the elaborate hierarchy of land rights, and of tenurial insecurity hurting production and accumulation incentives for the direct cultivator, has been cited as the block to agricultural progress. But even in some of these areas, the expansion of irrigation and public credit in recent years has unclogged the channels of productivity growth, at least for the rich and the middle farmers, and even in many traditional monsoon paddy regions the resulting rise in the production of, particularly, spring and summer crops has been significant. In the past, canal irrigation in the Punjab had created favourable preconditions for agricultural growth; in the rest of the country, where the dead weight of institutional legacy may have been more stifling, the 'pump-priming' role (to use an expression of old Keynesians in a different context) of public investment in stimulating growth is, and will remain, a matter of far greater importance. Even in Bihar and eastern Uttar Pradesh, which have been the graveyards of many economic planners' sturdiest hopes and which

---

million hectares, it is estimated that at current costs an additional investment of Rs 140 billion will be necessary. As for flood control, it has been estimated by the irrigation authorities that 80 per cent of the 40 million hectares of flood-prone areas are protectable, but only 12 million hectares have been protected so far.

together contain a population of about the size of the whole of Brazil, even in this vast area of darkness there is now plenty of scattered evidence that state and community projects for tapping groundwater through public tube-wells, for flood control and for soil improvements can have dramatic results. It should also be pointed out that in the high-rainfall regions of India, after centuries of agricultural involution and other related demographic-ecological processes, the average size of land holdings even among the better-off farmers is rather small (in contrast to the relatively large ones of north-western India), and as a result the size of investible surplus per farm is rather low. This makes the need for supplementary public investment and credit[7] all the more acute in these regions.

The preceding aruguments repeatedly emphasize the importance of public investment for agricultural growth. My purpose here is not merely to contrast this with the usual liberal emphasis on favourable price policy for farm products[8] and the usual radical emphasis on land reforms,[9] but more to link it up with the larger questions — which l take up later —

[7] In mid-1980 the total outstanding loans to agriculture per hectare of cropped area directly financed by scheduled commercial banks were almost three times as large in Punjab and Haryana taken together as in Bihar, Orissa and West Bengal taken together; the outstanding loans by primary agricultural credit societies and land development banks per hectare of cropped area were more than twice as large in the former region as in the latter.

[8] In contrast to the accumulated evidence for the sensitivity of inter-crop allocation of acreage to relative crop prices, there is very little hard evidence that agricultural output as a whole is significantly responsive to relative prices of agriculture to non-agriculture; in any case, the response to public investment in irrigation, etc., is much sharper.

[9] It is far from my intention to de-emphasize the importance of land reforms in servicing the cause of economic growth, apart from that of equity. Land redistribution and effective implementation of protective tenancy legislation can improve incentives for small framers, bring about a fuller utilization of their non-marketed family resources and improve their collaterals for credit. But such land reforms, if carried out in a piecemeal way, without the simultaneous activation of a public or community network of credit, input supplies, extension services, marketing and infrastructural facilities, may actually backfire. Besides, in

14

of the political economy of public investment and the nature of the state.

Public management of agricultural infrastructure is as (in the short to medium run, probably more) important as public investment. A large part of the irrigation potential created often remains underutilized. Apart from major problems with the management of the main canal systems, with the structure and practices of the irrigation bureaucracy, and with their insensitivity to local needs, in most areas there is no local corporate body or community organization to look after common water management problems of farmers below the outlet level; this frequently results in an anarchical water regime with serious shortages and irregular supplies, particularly for tail-end farmers. Here, possibly more than on the commonly discussed issue of land tenure and agricultural productivity, the institutional and organizational constraints are particularly severe. The full growth potential in Indian agriculture cannot be realized, even if resources for the requisite massive investments can be mobilized, until local broad-based community organizations (which can rise above or supersede conflicting individual property interests of landlords and 'waterlords' and internalise the considerable externalities) are developed not merely for the maintenance of field channels and drainage ditches and the allocation of water, but also for land shaping, the consolidation of highly fragmented holdings, flood control, the prevention of deforestation and soil erosion, and the like.[10]

---

a country where in large, densely populated areas the 'surplus' land at the top to be redistributed to the bottom is relatively small and where the inexorable opertion of subdivision and fragmentation through inheritance practices tends to push small land holdings towards uneconomic cultivation, land reforms without community organizations for pooling resources and risks, and without the cooperativization of services, if not of actual cultivation, may ultimately be self-defeating.

[10] For an elaboration of this agrument, see my 'Private Property as a Growth Constraint in a Hydraulic Economy' in Bardhan (1984).

One other feature of recent agricultural growth is striking. The variation around the trend growth rate is significantly higher in the second period than in the first, especially with respect to output of cereals.[11] A detailed statistical analysis[12] suggests that one primary reason for this is a greater synchronization of crop area and yield movements in different regions in the second period. In other words, output variability was relatively low in the first period because either area changes offset yield changes or increase in output of one crop offset the fall in output of another crop or increase in output of one region offset the fall in output in another. These offsetting movements declined considerably in the second period as a result of agriculture's increased dependence on purchased non-agricultural inputs which were subject to considerable supply instability. Supply fluctuations in fertilizers and electric power for irrigation pumps, for example, often affect many regions and crops simultaneously. Another likely reason for increased output instability may have to do with the increased incidence of floods affecting larger areas, presumably due to deforestation and soil erosion (on the basis of five-year moving-average data it has been estimated[13] that the proportion of total cropped area that was affected by floods towards the end of the seventies is about twice as large as that in the mid-fifties).

[11] See Mehra (1981).
[12] See Hazell (1982).
[13] This is reported in CMIE (1982).

3

Deceleration
in Industrial Growth

Let us now turn to industrial growth. The first point to note is that in spite of an impressive expansion over the years in the range and sophistication of output of manufactured goods, the manufacturing sector is still a relatively small part of the economy. As Table 5 shows, in 1981–82 the proportion contributed by the manufacturing sector to the net domestic product (at factor cost and at 1970–71 prices) was 15 per cent. This represents a small rise in the proportion, from around 12 per cent at the end of the 1950s. In fact it is remarkable that the contribution of the registered[1] part of the manufacturing sector is less than that of the sector categorized in national income accounts as trade, hotels and restaurants; this was so at the beginning of the 1950s, and this is still the case at the beginning of the 1980s.

Turning to rates of growth, calculated on the basis of disaggregated national accounts data[2] for value added at

[1] All factories employing 10 or more workers and using power, or more than 25 workers without power, are required to register.

[2] National accounts data for value added in the total manufacturing sector at constant prices are provided in Table 5. But for calculating the rate of growth for the period from 1956–57 to 1965–66 for the registered manufacturing sector, we have used the modified series of value added as used by Ahluwalia, I. (1983)

constant 1970–71 prices, the annual growth rate in the registered manufacturing sector was 6.9 per cent in the period from 1956–57 to 1965–66; this rate was 5.0 per cent in the period from 1966–67 to 1981–82, and this deceleration in the estimated growth rate in the second period is statistically significant.

Table 8 (based on I. Ahluwalia's analysis of the individual components of the manufacturing sector) shows that the only industry groups (at the two-digit level of disaggregation) with a statistically significant acceleration in its rate of growth in the second period are those of petroleum products and textiles. All other industry groups showed either significant deceleration or no significant change in the second period. The industries that showed substantial deceleration included mostly heavy industries, such as basic metals, metal products, machinery (both electrical and non-electrical) and transport equipment. While it is indeed an impressive index of structural change in Indian industries that these basic and capital goods industries (including electricity and mining) now account for nearly 50 per cent of total net value added in industry at 1970–71 prices (compared to 38 per cent in 1960–61), it is a matter of concern that the growth rates of value added for these industries were more than halved in the second part of the last three decades compared to the first. Consumer goods and intermediate goods industries, on the other hand, did not suffer from any significant deceleration in the growth rates of their value added, although these rates were maintained at rather low levels compared to those in basic and capital goods industries.

---

to take care of some problems of comparability with the data for the later period. One should also note here that we have used the national accounts value added data for the manufacturing sector in preference to the official indices of industrial production on account of problems of non-response, inadequate coverage and underreporting that afflict the latter. For a discussion of the differences in the patterns of growth rates based on these two alternative sources of industrial data, see Ahluwalia, I. (1983).

Some economists[3] have tried to explain the deceleration in the industrial growth rate in the second period in terms of increasing income inequality and the consequent limitation on the expansion of markets for mass consumer goods. I find this argument unsatisfactory, partly because the evidence on income or expenditure inequality is mixed and does not suggest any clear-cut increase over the years,[4] and partly because the growth deceleration in question does not seem to apply to consumer goods industries, as we have just noted from the disaggregated data. Textiles, the industry group that predominates among consumer goods industries, had actually a significant rise in the value-added growth rate from 2.3 per cent in the period of 1956–57 to 1965–66 to 4.3 per cent in the second period of 1966–67 to 1979–80 (with very large fluctuations in the growth rate in the 1970s). Among consumer goods industries, durables, of course, grew at a much faster rate than non-durables, but there was no statistically significant change in the growth rates of the former between the two periods.

The question of deceleration apart, there is no doubt that the growth rate in consumer goods industries (particularly non-durable) has been rather low (around 4 per cent annual growth in value added) over the last three decades. The relatively narrow base of the home market for industrial consumer goods may be an important factor here. This market is highly concentrated in the upper income groups. Estimates[5] from NSS data (at constant 1964–65 prices) indicate that in 1960–61 the bottom half of the rural popu-

---

[3] See, for example, Nayyar (1978).

[4] The estimates of Gini coefficients based on NSS data since the mid-sixties actually show some decline in inequality. But before rushing to conclusions, one should take into account the fact that these estimates are at current prices (whereas costs of living may have changed differentially for different groups) and that there is some suspicion that the proportion of unreported consumption of the rich in NSS consumption surveys may have increased over time.

[5] See Rangarajan (1982b) for the estimates.

lation together accounted for only 19 per cent of total rural consumption of industrial goods — industrial consumption goods comprising the categories described in NSS data as clothing, footwear, fuel and light, durables and miscellaneous goods and services. The top two deciles of the rural population, on the other hand, accounted for 55 per cent of the rural consumption of these industrial goods. In the urban sector, the shares are almost identical: the bottom half of the population accounting for 19 per cent and the top two deciles for 54 per cent of total consumption of industrial goods in that sector. These proportionate shares had hardly changed by 1973–74, when the bottom half of the population accounted for 21 per cent of industrial consumption in the rural sector and 20 per cent in the urban sector, and the top two deciles for 53 per cent in the rural sector and 54 per cent in the urban sector. These figures probably represent an underestimation of the actual concentration in industrial consumption since, as we have noted before, the NSS may not have adequately captured the consumption of very rich households.

A home market concentrated in the upper-income segments of the population is, of course, not necessarily a constraint on the rate of industrial growth. If exports expand sufficiently, or if the rich get richer at a sufficiently rapid rate and spend their booming income on 'luxury' consumption and reinvest their profits, industrial growth may not be broad-based or wholesome, but it can be fast,[6] as the recent history of countries like South Korea or Brazil has shown us. In the case of India, the performance in industrial exports, though it showed significant improvement in the 1970s compared to the earlier decades, has been relatively unexciting. India's

[6] For a formal theoretical macroeconomic model showing how increased income inequality may induce faster growth (if the investment response of 'luxury'-sector capitalists to higher profits is strong enough), see Taylor (1983, p. 175).

share in most exports in world trade, both traditional and non-traditional, has declined steadily over the last three decades, suggesting that by and large foreign demand was not the major constraint on the growth of exports. It should, however, be noted here that foreign trade as a proportion of national income, or luxury consumption as a proportion of total industrial consumer goods, is quantitatively so low in India that if expansion of exports or the production of luxury goods is to effectively pull up the rest of the economy by its bootstraps, this will involve a gigantic feat, more miraculous in dimensions than the South Korean or Brazilian 'miracle'.

Both from the demand side, in providing markets for consumer goods (like clothing and sugar) and intermediate goods (like fertilizers), and from the supply side, in providing raw materials (like cotton and sugar cane), the vast agricultural sector with it rather slow (and unstable) overall growth has had a dampening effect on the industrial growth rate,[7] particularly in consumer goods industries. An aggregative simulation model of the Indian economy[8] suggests that an increase in the growth rate of agricultural production by one per cent is likely to result, through all the direct and indirect demand and input linkage effects and the effects on savings and investments, in half a per cent rise in the rate of growth of industrial output (and a 0.7 per cent increase in the national income growth rate). Using the input-based classification of Indian industries, the growth rate over the last three decades in agro-based industries has been less than half of that in either metal-based or chemical-based industries, although the deceleration in the growth rate between the two periods under consideration has been sharpest in metal-based industries.

The idea of home-market demand constraining the rate of

---

[7] For an emphasis on this, see Vaidyanathan (1977).
[8] See Rangarajan (1982a) for such an exercise.

industrial growth is sometimes also expressed in the statement that by the middle of the 1960s, i.e. the end of our first period, the possibilities of import substitution (the policy which had been providing an automatic expansion of demand in some sectors) more or less exhausted themselves and that the constraint of home demand was more binding in the second period. It is true that the major high-growth industries (like machinery, chemicals and chemical products, paper and paper products, etc.) are usually in product groups where there was a relatively high import-to-availability ratio in the 1950s. But a study of the behaviour over time of this ratio by industry groups (see Table 9) suggests that significant growth deceleration in the second period has not been necessarily associated with the end of import substitution. We have already noted that growth deceleration was significant essentially in the basic and capital goods industries, yet the import-to-availability ratio in some of these industries, which declined over the first period, went on declining in the second period (although the rate of decline was faster in the first period than in the second for basic metals, metal products and transport equipment, but not for machinery industries). On the other hand, there were some industry groups (for example, food manufacturing or petroleum products) where there was no growth deceleration even though the import-to-availability ratio rose in the second period.

4

Public Investment
and Slow Economic Growth

The growth deceleration in basic and capital goods industries seems to be more strongly linked to a deceleration in public investment.[1] Investment generates demand for capital goods and in India public investment plays the leading role in this: in 1981–82 gross fixed capital formation in the public sector was nearly half of the corresponding total in the economy (see Table 10) and about five times the amount in the private corporate sector. Besides contributing to demand for capital goods, private investment adds to capacity creation in some vital sectors providing infrastructural inputs like power, fuel and transport, much of which is in the public sector. It is, therefore, important to note that there was a significant deceleration in the growth rate of public investment between the two periods under consideration. Fixed capital formation in the public sector at 1970–71 prices grew at the annual rate of 11.3 per cent in the period of 1950–51 to 1965–66, but in the second period of 1966–67 to 1981–82 it dropped to a rate which is less than half, 5.5 per cent. (This is actually an underestimate of the deceleration in the rate of public invest-

---

[1] For the first detailed exposition of this view, see Srinivasan and Narayana (1977).

ment, since in the second period some more industries came under the rubric of public sector through nationalization.) Since the mid-sixties the cutbacks in public investment in critical sectors like railways[2] and (up to the mid-seventies) electricity have been párticularly severe, with obvious consequences for industrial growth. The shortages in infrastructural sectors like power, fuel and transport have a cumulative impact much more drastic than what appears from a consideration of each individual sectoral shortage: a scarcity of wagons leads to inadequte delivery of coal from pit-heads to power-plants, the resultant deficient and erratic power supply damages as well as slows down coal-mining equipment and electric railway engines, and so on. In recent years the expansion of private trucking and installation of what are known as 'captive' private power-generating sets in industrial units[3] have marginally supplemented the transport and power needs respectively; but the former is often less fuel-efficient than railways, and the latter obviously does not have the scale economies of public electricity grids.

The rate of growth in private investment moved in sympathy with that in public investment, although not to the same extent. An econometric analysis[4] of the time-series

[2] On the basis of three-year moving average data, it is estimated that gross capital formation in railways as a proportion of total gross domestic capital formation at 1970–71 prices declined from 9 per cent in 1964–65 to 3.4 per cent in 1970–71 and to 3.3 per cent in 1980–81. As a result the annual growth rate of railway freight traffic (either in terms of tonnes originating or net tonne kilometres travelled) dropped substantially in the last fifteen years compared to the earlier period.

[3] In 1981 the share of non-utilities in electricity consumption was 7 per cent. The share is particularly high in industries like mineral oil, petrochemicals, sugar, etc. The share of goods traffic by rail has declined from 89 per cent in 1950–51 to 66 per cent in 1978–79.

[4] We tried a linear regression analysis with current private corporate investment each year at constant prices as the dependent variable, and, as explanatory variables, public investment of the previous year at constant prices, the ratio of wholesale price indices of agricultural to manufactured commodities of the

24

data (from 1951–52 to 1980–81) on investment suggests that the stimulation effect of public investment (through growth in demand for private industrial output and in supply of infrastructural inputs) on private (particularly corporate) investment tends to dominate any possible negative effect through competing for investible funds. The elasticity of private corporate investment with respect to public investment (of the previous year) is estimated to be as high as 0.73.

As Table 10 indicates, the rate of gross domestic saving as a percentage of the gross domestic product at current market prices rose from a little over 9 per cent in the early 1950s to over 15 per cent by the middle of the 1960s and to over 22 per cent at the beginning of the 1980s.[5] The rate of trans-

---

previous year (a proxy for inter-sectoral terms of trade), yearly changes in non-agricultural income at constant prices (a proxy for expected output changes), and the surplus of total savings (deflated by capital goods price deflator) over public investment of the current year at constant prices (a proxy for private investible surplus). Only the first explanatory variable turned out to be statistically significant. In another regression equation, we had current total private investment at constant prices as the dependent variable, and the same explanatory variables as in the earlier equation (except in the proxy variable for expected output changes we took yearly changes in national income rather than only non-agricultural income). This time, except for this variable for expected output changes, all the other three explanatory variables were statistically significant. The regression coefficient for the lagged public investment variable was 0.52, slightly exceeding that for the investible surplus variable, which was 0.49. It seems public investment does not 'crowd out' funds for investment in the private corporate sector, but it does draw upon the investible surplus of the household sector, including unincorporated enterprises, to be balanced by its stimulating effect on the latter. We may also note here that in an econometric model of the Indian economy Krishnamurthy and Saibaba (1983) observe that even when public investment crowds out private investment in some sectors and for some initial years, aggregate real gross domestic product does not suffer losses, public sector output replacing private output.

[5] This large rise in the savings rate (even after taking into account a differential price rise in capital goods) has not been adequately explained in the literature. One possible explanation is the very significant decline in the percentage share of agriculture in gross domestic product (by about one-third over the last thirty years) coupled with the presumption (supported by some household survey information) that the agricultural sector has a lower propensity to save. Rakshit

formation of savings into investment has, however, been seriously affected by the high rate of price rise in capital goods in recent years (see Table 12). If one looks at the data on the rate of gross fixed capital formation (both public and private) at constant 1970–71 prices as a percentage of the gross domestic product over the last thirty years, one deciphers some significant up-and-down movements. Even when one takes three-year moving averages to smooth annual fluctuations, one finds from Table 10 that this rate was slightly less than 15 per cent in the mid-fifties, climbed to its peak at nearly 18 per cent in 1966–67, then there was a fall in this rate until around 1974–75, since when it has started rising again, and in 1981–82 it was about 17 per cent, slightly below the peak reached in the mid-sixties. The general pattern of movement in the rate of gross fixed capital formation in the public sector was also very similar, rising to a peak in the mid-sixties, then, after declining for about a decade, climbing back in recent years to about the level of the earlier peak.

The rise in the public investment rate in very recent years, in spite of a sharp decline in the net inflow of foreign resources in the seventies (see Table 11), has been facilitated by large transfers of household-sector savings through the expansion of public financial intermediation in the form of nationalized banks and insurance companies, various schemes of compulsory savings for growing numbers of salaried employees in the public sector, and by the recent rise in revenues from increased prices of petroleum and other public-sector products. But, as we have noted above, the rate of public investment has yet to significantly exceed the peak of the mid-sixties,

---

(1982) has pointed out some sources of upward bias in the saving estimates (particularly with respect to financial saving of the household sector) and that this bias may have increased in recent years. One may also suggest that if the extent of differential underreporting in gross domestic product (induced by taxes, controls, etc.) has gone up, this may lead to an increasing upward bias in saving ratios.

and for the second half of the last three decades taken as a whole there has been a significant deceleration in public investment. This has been largely because the mounting current expenditures of the Government have steadily eaten away the bulk of the potentially investible resources that it mobilizes. We shall come back to analyse (in chapter 8) the political economy of the forces that generate these pressures on the current expenditures of the Government at the expense of public investment.

At the same time we should also note that a 17 per cent gross fixed capital formation rate (at 1970–71 prices) is 1981–82 is a relatively high rate for a poor country like India; it is more like the investment rates in middle-income or even some richer, industrialized countries. Why is it not being reflected in a respectable growth rate? One hypothesis[6] is in terms of an unusually high (and even rising) incremental capital–output ratio, namely that the effects of high investment are being partially cancelled by a low productivity of that investment. International comparisons of incremental capital–output ratios are tricky, but there is hardly any doubt that India has one of the highest ratios among developing countries.[7] Of course, it is true that in more recent years the pattern of investment within the large-scale industrial sector in India has shifted in favour of industries with relatively high capital–output ratios such as chemical fertilizers, petrochemicals, and electricity generation, transmission and distribution. But a disaggregated industry groupwise analysis[8] suggests that the rise in capital–output ratio characterizes almost all of the industry groups individually and is not just the outcome of a change in the composition of the aggregate industrial sector. In fact, there is some evidence to suggest that the contribution to the rise in capital–output ratio from

[6] For an emphasis on this, see Desai (1981).
[7] See, for example, World Bank (1983b, p. 61).
[8] See Ahluwalia, I. (1983).

across-the-board increases in individual industry groups dominates that from the change in the industrial output-mix.

Capital–output ratios in individual industries have been rising sharply in many parts of the world, including the industrially advanced countries, particularly after the phenomenal fuel price rises of the seventies. In India the rise in the relative price of capital goods in recent years, which we have noted above, may have contributed to the rise in capital-output ratios. All this may have been reinforced by the fact that, after the exhaustion of easier forms of economic expansion in initial years, some of the technically more complex and costly forms of capacity creation even within the same industry group may have been unavoidable. Even outside the industrial sector, in irrigation, for example, it has been estimated that over the last thirty years, as water-wise more intractable territories are being explored, the cost per hectare of creating irrigation potential has doubled even at constant prices. Nevertheless, there is no doubt that a major part of the general rise in capital–output ratio in India is attributable to the inefficiency in utilization and management of capital. In the literature on import-substituting industrialization, many liberal economists have pointed to the manifold inefficiencies arising from the bureaucratic allocation mechanisms of restrictive foreign-trade regimes.[9] While, clearly, such a regime in India has sheltered many white elephants in the industrial sector and lined many pockets in the corridors of power, the overall dynamic impact of import-substitution in fostering skill-formation and learning-by-doing in a whole range of sophisticated manufacturing industries (producing engineering, machinery, chemical and other products) may not have been negligible, although at a very high immediate cost to consumers and

[9] For one of the most well-known accounts in the case of India, see Bhagwati and Srinivasan (1975).

28

industrial users of domestic intermediate and capital goods. Systematic quantitative estimates of learning effects induced by import-substitution are scarce, although there are some scattered studies in individual industries (fertilizers, auto-assembly and components, and so on) and indirect evidence from some modest success in exports of capital goods and other manufactures to low and middle-income countries. This, of course, does not justify the blanket policy of automatic protection (or its specific form in terms of quantitative rather than tariff restrictions) – without regard to current or expected cost advantages – which most industries have received, at least up to the mid-seventies, and which has contributed to inefficiency and high capital–output ratios all around. At the same time, the effect of high capital-output ratios on the aggregate economic growth may have been partially neutralized by the likely effect of import-substitution in raising the rate of saving and investment in the economy (given the differential propensities to save and invest of the industrial as opposed to the agricultural sector, of corporate as opposed to unincorporated enterprises). In any case, the Indian trade regime has not by and large been more restrictive in the second period under consideration than in the first (if anything, the trend has been towards greater liberalization in recent years)[10] and hence this may not be a good explanation of the industrial deceleration in the second period.

The rise in capital–output ratios is particularly prominent in the industries belonging to the public sector, and in industries where both the public and private sectors coexist,

---

[10] Since 1975 a very large number of capital goods and industrial inputs (affecting more than half of imports at present) has been added to the so-called 'open' general licence (OGL) and 'free' licence lists (even though some restrictions in the form of 'actual user' or 'eligible importer' qualifications and canalization through public enterprises remain), in general gradually moving towards a tariff system from a quota-bound import policy.

being larger in the former than in the latter. The available estimates of capacity utilization are extremely low for electricity generation (which is almost entirely in the public sector), and in other key sectors like basic metals including steel, non-electrical machinery and transport equipment (which are all dominated by public enterprises). In the sectors where public and private ownership coexist, capacity utilization is often lower in the former by 15 to 20 percentage points. In 1982–83, out of 164 productive units in the public sector under the Central Government for which data were available from the Bureau of Public Enterprises, 74 (i.e. 45 per cent) reported capacity utilization below 75 per cent and 31 reported utilization even below 50 per cent. The situation in units under the State Governments is usually more worse. While some of these capacity utilization problems arise from lack of complementary investments and other technological bottlenecks and demand deficiencies emanating from a slowing down of public investment growth (particularly in the case of machinery industries), much of it is no doubt, due to political and administrative mismanagement.

Capital–output ratios have been inflated also (often primarily) by increasingly frequent cases of long lags in the construction of new capacity in the public sector (on steel, railway, power, irrigation and other projects) resulting in a drastic escalation of capital costs. The details of project costs published by the Government and the public financial institutions suggest that a significant and rising proportion of project costs are absorbed in items other than fixed assets. The estimates of cost escalations run into several billions of rupees even in single projects.[11] Here, irresponsible political

---

[11] For exaples of major cost escalations, let us quote from Krishna (1984, p. 65):

According to information available about projects in key sectors, only 42 out of 192 major irrigation projects undertaken in the 30 years (1951–80) have been completed so far, and long construction lags have already

decision-taking in initiating a project is often as much responsible as delays due to technical or administrative reasons.
I shall come back (in chapter 8) to the politics of rising
capital–output ratios when I consider the nature of the state
in more detail.

---

doubled the investment cost of the unfinished projects. In 66 projects the
extra cost has already added up to Rs 50 billion. In 150 major and 30,000
minor irrigation projects lags have ranged between 2 and 25 years. Two
major steel plant expansion projects (Bhilai and Bokaro) are expected to
be completed 4 to 5 years late; the extra cost exceeds Rs 12 billion.

In the vital atomic energy sector, the construction lag has been 2 to 7
years and the extra cost nearly Rs 3 billion, or more than half the original
estimate. Major coal projects are moving 1 to 4 years late, and 5 major
thermal power projects in the northern region 7 to 45 months late. Similar
delays and cost-overruns characterize major projects in many sectors: non-
ferrous metals, cement, paper, fertilizer, engineering, and oil-refining. The
average annual cost-overruns and associated losses in industrial projects in
the 1970s are estimated to be Rs 10 billion.

5

The State as an
Autonomous Actor

We now turn from the world of economic statistics to that of political sociology, and focus our attention on the broad nature of the Indian state. The orthodox Marxist view, in India as elsewhere, is to treat the Government as 'a committee for managing the common affairs' of the dominant proprietory class in society, to take the state in a capitalist society, for example, as a direct tool of the capitalist class. There is strong evidence to believe that Marx himself essentially abandoned this view after 1850, after the disappointments of the revolutions of 1848. To quote Eric Hobsbawm (1982): 'The bourgeois revolution had failed in 1848 or led to unpredicted regimes whose nature probably preoccupied Marx more than any other problem concerning the bourgeois state: to states plainly serving the bourgeoisie's interest, but not directly representing it as a class.' Shortly afterwards, in his discussion of France under Louis Bonaparte in the *Eighteenth Brumaire* and of British politics in a couple of articles published in the *New York Daily Tribune* around the same time, Marx developed a somewhat more complex theory,[1] according to which the bourgeoisie voluntarily

---

[1] For an exposition of this interpretation, see Elster (1984, ch. 7).

abdicate from power (as in the contemporary Bonapartist regime of France) or abstain from taking it (as in England under the Whigs) because they perceive that their interests may be better served by remaining outside politics. This is the origin of the neo-Marxist idea of the state being 'relatively autonomous' of the dominant economic class even though it acts on behalf of the latter and safeguards its interests.[2] To secure the *general* and long-run interests of the dominant class and its hegemony over the dominated classes, it may be necessary for the state to acquire freedom of action or functional autonomy with regard to the *particular* and short-run interests of individual parts of the dominant class. One also recalls how Marx in *Das Kapital* (Vol. I), in his analysis of English Factory Acts, deduces the necessity of the state as a particular form 'alongside and outside bourgeois society' protecting capital from its own 'unrestrainable passion, its werewolf hunger for surplus labour'.

This 'relative autonomy', the state acting not *at the behest of*, but for all practical purposes *on behalf of* the dominant proprietary class is, however, highly inadequate, and even misleading, in capturing the dynamics of state action in the process of industrialization in the last hundred years or so. The society-centered theories of politics and government of the orthodox Marxists as well as the liberal-pluralists and structural-functionalists have managed to keep our eyes averted from what Skocpol (1982) calls 'the explanatory centrality of states as potent and autonomous organizational actors'. There are, of course, serious constraints posed by the imperatives of the dominant proprietary class, but to focus exclusively on them is to ignore the large range of choices in goal formulation, agenda setting and policy execution that the state leadership usually has, and the powerful impulses shaping policies and actions that are

---

[2] The most well-known exponent of this idea is Poulantzas (1973).

33

generated *within* the state, fueled not merely by motives of self-aggrandizement but quite often also by what Miliband (1983) calls its 'conception of the national interest'. In many cases of state-directed industrialization, the leadership genuinely considers itself as the trustee of the nation's most deeply held normative aspirations,[3] and in a world of international military and economic competition, these aspirations often taks the form of striving for rapid economic growth. Engels in a letter (to Danielson) in 1892, while discussing the role of the Russian absolutist state in industrialization, writes: 'All governments, be they ever so absolute, are *en dernier lieu* but the executors of the economic necessities of the national situation.' Mark the emphasis on national rather than class necessities.

Perhaps the most dramatically successful case of the state as the executor of national economic aspirations with a revolution from above is that of Japan after the Meiji Restoration. The Meiji state was not just a reflection of the pressures exerted by the existing dominant classes in society. The state elite, drawn from the periphery of these classes, believed that the Western military and economic challenge demanded a fundamental restructuring of Japanese civil society. A series of policies and reforms were forcefully carried out from above which undermined the position of the nobility, centralized the political and economic administration and imposed Western technological and organizational structures.[4] Of course, clever functionalist hindsight will

---

[3] The normative aspects of these aspirations have been emphasized in the 'organic-static' approach to the state in the Latin American context by Stepan (1978).

[4] For a persuasive recent presentation of this view, see Trimberger (1978). Some scholars have pointed to the rising influence of the rich peasants (the *gono*) in this period, and there are differences of opinion about the relative importance of the power of the Meiji bureaucrats as opposed to that of this landed class. While the political influence of the *gono* increased over time, it is probably correct to say that the small group of samurai bureaucrats who led

34

tell us that the state was only doing the job on behalf of the rising bourgeoisie. But such convenient telelogy is no substitute for explanation. Marxists have to recognize the ways in which the state occasionally shapes class realignments in civil society, and wields the midwife's knife in the birth of some new classes. Engels actually went a step farther; in 1890, while discussing the impact of the defeats in the Crimean War on the Russian state, he writes:[5] 'The war had proved that Russia needed railways, steam engines, modern industry, even on purely military grounds. And thus the government set about *breeding* [emphasis mine] a Russian capitalist class ... The new development of the bourgeoisie was artificially forced as in a hot-house, by means of railway concessions, protective duties, and other privileges.' In this he was echoing Marx, who in a letter (to Vera Zasulich) in 1881 states that 'the [Russian] state has hothouse-forced the growth of branches of the Western capitalist system'.

The state not merely shapes class realignments or provides the material basis for new classes; in many newly industrializing countries, the state is today an important part of the economic base itself. When from 1853 onwards Marx and Engels first started discussing the problems of 'Asiatic' societies, they developed, as Gouldner (1980) emphasizes, a theory of the state that went far beyond their primary paradigm: the state now owned means of production (land), constructing and managing large-scale irrigation works essential for agriculture in arid climates, and the agro-managerial bureaucracy exerted control over all proprietary classes in society. We need not concern ourselves here with the fact

the Meiji Restoration retained control of the state apparatus for a long enough time to give a distinctive leadership to the early stages of the process of industrialization.

[5] This quotation from a magazine article by Engels, 'The Foreign Policy of Russian Czarism', May 1890, has been cited by Draper (1977).

that Marx and Engels were not particularly well informed about Asian history, or that the historical basis is extremely shaky for the idea of an absence of private property in land in Asia or for that of the hydraulic state exercising complete control over labour power, particularly as enunciated in the drastic generalizations of Wittfogel. But the idea of a centralized powerful state, combining its monopoly of the means of repression with a substantial ownership in the means of production, propelling as well as regulating the economy, which is implicit[6] in the writings of Marx and Engels on Asiatic societies, has widespread contemporary relevance beyond the exotic, little-understood, precapitalist social formations to which many western Marxists would like to keep it confined. The recent experience of technocratic and entrepreneurial states in the dynamic capitalist societies of Japan, South Korea, Brazil and others, and the challenge they have posed to the older industrial economies, suggest that the role of the state in large-scale irrigation works, central to the Asiatic mode of production, with their externalities and indivisibilities (not easily appropriable in private market arrangements) and with the protective and developmental functions they serve for an agrarian society, is not *in principle* remote from the pioneering and catalytic role of the state in those recent cases of industrial-technological transformation. The state often has a large stake in capital formation (as, for example, in Brazil or South Korea where a predominant part of total investment in the economy is in the public sector), and (as in the well-known, widely envied example of the Ministry of International Trade and Industry

---

[6] It is, of course, necessary to point out that Marx himself largely shared the anti-etatist views of the nineteenth-century liberals. He found in the Asiatic state, with its monopoly of economic initiative, an explanation for the backwardness of the East. But it is possible to reorient the argument in a different context with a different historical dynamic of state entrepreneurship.

in Japan) in long-range planning, promotion, risk-taking and credit-supply.

In countries of delayed industrialization, the state has usually played a more active role, as the history of south, central and eastern parts of Europe, as contrasted with the western, clearly shows. But in the developing countries today, where in particular the private capital markets and the insurance markets are extremely inadequately developed, the state is often the only agency which can provide the capital and underwrite the risks involved in large initial investment ventures in the early stage of industrialization. The problems of market failure, fragmentation, and even non-existence in credit and insurance markets are qualitatively similar to the problems of externalities and indivisibilities in large-scale irrigation and flood-control programmes which necessitate state participation in agrarian development. Even in late stages of industrialization the success story of Japan underlines the imperative of state leadership in restructuring the economy in pace with the rapidly changing technological frontier, in raising and re-allocating massive amounts of long-term industrial finance and in underwriting the risks of innovations.

In India, irrespective of the exigencies of delayed industrialization, the civil society was already dominated by a relatively overdeveloped state at the time of Independence (overdeveloped in relation to the economic structure). Some Marxist scholars[7] have traced the extraordinary powers of control and regulation vested in the state to the colonial administration ruling an alien land. But this overdeveloped state actually goes back to pre-colonial days and was certainly evident during the peak of the Moghal rule in India. There is, however, no question that over the last three decades the state has accumulated powers of direct ownership and

[7] For example, Alavi (1972).

37

control in the economy to an extent unparalleled in Indian history, both in the spheres of circulation (banking, credit, transport, distribution and foreign trade) and of production — directly manufacturing much of basic and capital goods, owning more than 60 per cent of all productive capital in the industrial sector (see Table 13), running 8 of the top 10 industrial units in the country (see Table 14), directly employing two-thirds of all workers in the organized sector, holding through nationalized financial institutions more than 25 per cent of paid-up capital of joint-stock companies in the private sector (this proportion much higher in new companies), and regulating patterns of private investment down to industrial product level and choice of technology extending to scale, location and import-content. The state elite that inherited the power at the time of Independence enjoyed enormous prestige and a sufficiently unified sense of ideological purpose about the desirability of using state intervention to promote national economic development; it redirected and restructured the economy, and in the process exerted great pressure on the proprietary classes. This led to considerable complexity and fluidity in the composition of the proprietary classes and their relationship with the state. But while the state elite from its commanding heights formulated goals and pointed policy directions, neither at the behest of nor on behalf of the proprietary classes, it could not ignore the serious constraints on the framework of policy actions and certainly on their effective implementation posed by the articulated interests of those classes; and as the aura of special legitimacy of leaders derived from their participation in the freedom movement and from serving in British prisons waned in the wheeling-dealing of day-to-day post-Independence politics (and as some of the widely respected figures of that generation passed away), they could get away with fewer and fewer of the autonomous policy directives, and the constraints

38

became binding. Furthermore, as we shall see in Chapter 8, the plurality of these constraints and the complexity of their mutual interaction in a noisy open polity have generated pressures which have seriously interfered with the accumulation and management functions of the public economy. As a consequence, the autonomy of the Indian state is reflected more often in its regulatory (and hence patronage-dispensing) than developmental role.

6

The Dominant
Proprietary Classes

Let us now look at the dominant proprietary classes. The first thing that strikes one in this respect in the Indian scene is the plurality and heterogeneity of these classes, and the conflicts in their interests are sufficiently important not to make this comparable to the division of the bourgeoisie in industrially advanced countries into different, largely complementary, 'fractions', like industrial capital, finance capital and mercantile capital. The industrial capitalist class, mainly under the leadership of some of the top business families from western India, was reasonably strong at the time of Independence. It supported the government policy of encouraging import-substituting industrialization, quantitative trade restrictions providing automatically protected domestic markets, and of running a large public sector providing capital goods, intermediate products and infrastructural facilities for private industry, often at artificially low prices. Since the mid-fifties, the government has created several public lending institutions, loans from which form the predominant source of private industrial finance (in contrast with the 'internal financing' from undistributed profits in industrially advanced countries).[1] Even the ostensibly adverse government policy of an elaborate scheme of industrial and import licences has been allowed to be turned to the advantage of the industrial and commerical interests they were designed to control: the richer industrialists, having better 'connections' and better access, have got away with the lion's share in the bureaucratic allocations of the licences, thus pre-empting capacity creation and sheltering oligopolistic profits. In cases where licensing regulations have been directly aimed at them, the big industrial houses have often freely violated these regulations, created unlicensed capacities (as, for example, in 46 units of the Birla group alone) and produced far in excess of the quantity permitted. Over the last decades there has not been a single case of any such company being prosecuted for such violations;[2] on the contrary, repeatedly the Government has *ex post* regularized their unauthorized capacity creation. In the last couple of years many of the regulations themselves have been taken away or watered down. Similarly, the major potential threat of converting loans from public financial institutions into equity in the private companies has now been diluted. But even in cases where these financial institutions have held substantial equities, by and large they have played a passive role, not interfering with the family control of the business houses in spite of many cases of indifferent management. The controlling interest of the public financial institutions in companies has been used more often to take over 'sick' or marginal units saddled with large losses. Thus the govern-

[1] It is estimated from Reserve Bank data that in large private sector companies the share of internal source of finance for their gross assets formation declined from 55 per cent in the early sixties to about 40 per cent at the end of the seventies.

[2] In a meeting with the then Minister for Industries in the mid-seventies, H.P. Nanda, chairman of Escorts Ltd, is reported to have challenged: 'If there is a market, and if I can produce to feed the market, I will not allow your licensing regulations to come in my way. If you penalize me for this, I will not pay the fine. Please come and arrest me.'

ment not merely finances private industry, it also acts as the risk-absorber of the last resort and a charitable hospital where the private sector can dump its sick units.

In 1976 the top 20 business houses are reported to have controlled nearly two-thirds of the total productive capital in the private corporate sector. This concentration of assets may not have diminished in recent years, as even the pretence of government control over monopoly houses has been more or less given up since the mid-seventies, and also there has been a spate of company take-overs in recent years. On account of the problems of pricing assets, valuing stocks and computing for depreciation, sales volume may be a more reliable indicator than assets of the economic importance of the top 20 houses. (In any case the top business houses now control essentially through management, not majority owner-ship.) Table 15 suggests that their sales as a proportion of net domestic product in the private organized sector at current prices grew about one and a half times over the seventies.

While the private industrial pyramid remains concentrated at the top, over the last decade or so there have been some dramatic changes in the composition of the list of top business houses. While the supremacy of the Birlas and the Tatas remain unchallenged (115 companies controlled by them accounting for nearly 40 per cent of all sales of the top 20 industrial houses), the fastest growing business groups are somewhat lower down in the list: like Ambani (who converted his windfall profits from trading premia-fetching import entitlements into industrial capital and whose Reliance Textile Industries Ltd, with sales multiplying 33 times in just one decade, is set to become the largest textile unit in the country, and by the end of 1982 is the sixth largest among all private industrial companies, yielding precedence only to such vintage ventures as Telco, Tata Steel, ITC, DCM, and Hindusthan Lever); the Modis (whose sales in a well-diversified group of industries multiplied eightfold in as many years); Nanda (the automotive tycoon whose sales multiplied sixfold in nine years); and so on. Some of these up-coming companies have also been the quicket in taking advantage of the recent easing of restrictions on foreign collaborations and in forging links with transnational companies.

Another feature of the changing organization of industrial capital is the substantial expansion of small-scale industries and a possibly increased incidence of subcontracting and ancillarization. Even though the evidence for the factory sector (shown in Table 16) from the Annual Survey of Industries suggests that in 1978–79 the officially defined small-scale sector (plant and machinery up to Rs 1 million) accounted for only 7.5 per cent of productive capital and 14.5 per cent of value added, looking at factory starting dates it is found that of all factories that started production between 1966 and 1978 nearly half was in the small-scale sector, accounting for 30 per cent of productive capital and 25 per cent of value added. The share of individual proprietors and private partnerships in the total stock of capital within privately owned enterprises in the factory sector steadily rose over the seventies. While the coverage of small-scale units of the Annual Survey of Industries has been incomplete and variable, and while many of the registered small units are fictitious entities to take advantage of the exemptions (from regulations and taxes) and benefits these units enjoy, there is no doubt that there has been a remarkable growth in the number and activity of small units (for example, in textiles with powerlooms, leather products, etc.), particularly where there have been serious restrictions on the output of the large-scale units in many products (the number of products reserved exclusively for the small-scale sector rose from 128 in Februrary 1971 to 844 by August 1981). Many of the small units are actually owned by large business houses;[3]

[3] It has been reported, for example, that J.K. Helene Curtis, a small-scale unit, is owned by the Sanghania group; small units like Dental Products of India

there is also some fragmentary evidence pointing to growing ancillarization (in engineering industries, for example). Subcontracting and ancillarization not merely help large companies avoid excise taxes and labour laws, they also line up for them numerically strong vertical alliances that may prove politically useful in putting pressure on the government. Of course, not all small-scale units are satellites of large units, and the expansion in their number indicates some lengthening of the 'tail' of distribution of firms in many industries. To the extent the generation or acquisition of new technology is strongly related to scale economies, the long-tailed market structure in many industries may be a factor slowing down technological progress in the private sector.[4]

In contrast to many Latin American countries, where a major focus of analysis of the capitalist structure is on the role of international capital (primarily embodied in trans-national corporations) and its interaction with a relatively weak local bourgeoisie, a remarkable feature of Indian development is the relative unimportance of foreign capital and foreign firms. CMIE (1983) has estimated that in 1981–82 only about 10 per cent of total value added in the factory sector of mining and manufacturing was accounted for by foreign firms[5] (even taking into consideration only very large firms with sales exceeding Rs 0.41 billion, the foreign firms accounted for less than 13 per cent of their value

---

or Vitro-Pharma Products belong to Shaw Wallace; Indian National Diesel Co. is owned by Mahindra; Ewac Alloys by Larsen and Toubro; Garment Enterprises by Finlay; and so on.

[4] This is hypothesized by Desai (1982). He notes that between 1963–64 and 1978–79 the Herfindahl index fell in most industries in the set of engineering, electrical and vehicle industry groups that he considers, even though the index of inequality of firm size did not, indicating generally a rise in the number of firms.

[5] Strictly speaking the FERA (Foreign Exchange Regulation Act) units, including also those units which have diluted their foreign share-holding in recent years in view of this Act.

added). While their average presence is low, the foreign enterprises, however, have high market shares in a very small number of industries: it is about 50 per cent or more in industries producing cigarettes, soap and detergents, typewriters, electrodes, glycerine, explosives, batteries and bulbs. Of the top 25 industrial units of India listed in Table 14, only 4 are foreign: Hindusthan Lever, Indian Tobacco, Ashok Leyland, and Dunlop. Some of these large foreign firms have retained their pre-eminence for several decades primarily through their advantage in marketing organization and adaptability, while most other colonial firms declined. In the newer, more technology-intensive industries, foreign firms have only a minor role. After Independence many of the foreign branch-companies (mainly in plantations, mines and services) were sold off to Indian businessmen; then, with the onset of the regime of import-substitution, foreign companies set up manufacturing subsidiaries to protect their market shares (especially in chemicals and pharmaceuticals); but since the mid-sixties the government licensing policy and regulations on foreign share-holding have seriously discouraged foreign investment. New foreign private direct investment has been minimal: in spite of a significant increase in foreign collaboration agreements in recent years, the overwhelming proportion of such agreements do not involve any foreign participation in equity capital.[6] Most technology imports have now been through outright purchase arrangements, after the decline of the importance of licensing agreements induced by the government policy of controls on royalties and of regulations aimed at reducing the dependence of local producers on the technology suppliers.

From the industrial bourgeoisie let me now turn to *numerically* the most important proprietary class, that of rich

---

[6] Desai (1983) estimates that in 1977–80 86.5 per cent of technology import agreements did not involve any foreign share of equity capital.

farmers. The immediate post-Independence land reforms accelerated the already on-going process of the transfer of land from non-cultivating, absentee, often upper-caste landlords (who had been moving into the professions and services for several decades) to enterprising rich farmers often belonging to the middle castes, and in some cases the erstwhile landlords now found it profitable to convert themselves into big farmers with the use of hired labourers and sharecroppers. The Government has assured for these rich farmers substantial price support for farm products (particularly since the mid-sixties) and liberal provision of subsidized inputs (water, power, fertilizers, diesel, tractors, etc.) and institutional credit. Agriculture is in the constitutional domain of the State Governments, but with the power of rich farmers being more of a direct constraint on them than on the Central Government, there has been hardly any significant taxation of agricultural income and wealth.

Empirical identification of the class of rich farmers is, of course, arbitrary, largely depending on the purpose for which such classification is used. Table 17 suggests that large and very large farm households, cultivating holdings above 4 hectares, constituting 19 per cent of rural agricultural population, accounted for 60 per cent of cultivated area and 53 per cent of crop output in 1975. On account of land quality variations and the varying importance of other assets like livestock and buildings, asset distribution data may be more significant than land distribution data. The All-India Debt and Investment Survey data on rural asset distribution collected by the Reserve Bank of India show that in 1971 about 20 per cent of cultivator households, owning more than Rs 20,000 in assets, accounted for 63 per cent of all rural assets. This estimate is an average for rural India, and it varies substantially from one region to another; Table 18 indicates that in Punjab, for example, 73 per cent of all rural households owned more than Rs 20,000 in assets, while in Orissa the corresponding propottion was less than 7 per cent. In the orthodox Marxist way of analysing the class structure, one, of course, does not look just at the asset distribution pattern, but tries to identify the rich farmers as those who hire labour power and 'exploit' the agricultural proletariat. Unfortunately, there are no quantitative estimates of rich farmers defined in this way at the aggregative all-India level. On the basis of retabulation of some NSS data, I have worked out such an estimate of rich farmers for rural West Bengal:[7] in 1972–73 16 per cent of all rural households deriving their income primarily from agricultural occupations were rich farmers in the sense of being net hirers of wage labour. Since the extent of labour hiring is larger in densely populated West Bengal than in, say, large parts of North or Central India, the all-India proportion for rich farmers in this sense may be somewhat lower. But I doubt if, for our present purpose of identifying the class of rich farmers as posing a serious constraint on the policy actions of the state, the orthodox Marxist definition based on the criterion of labour hiring and surplus value extraction is as yet of much significance. Except in localized pockets, the exploited poor peasants and agricultural wage labourers are still highly unorganized and often locked into dyadic and clientelist relationships with the rich farmers, their employer-creditors, and far from being a 'class for itself'. More often than not they have been mobilized and harnessed by rich farmers in large-scale rural movements which serve primarily the latters' class interests – in agitations for lower taxes, higher prices, and better subsidies. The intermediate class of primarily family farmers is also a willing ally of rich farmers in these movements; it gains from lower irrigation and power rates, higher prices for farm products and subsidized credit and inputs like fertilizers, even though the benefits go dispropor-

[7] See Bardhan (1982).

tionately to the rich farmers. On state policies affecting agriculture there are no serious conflicts of interests between rich farmers and family farmers; the conflicts are potentially more antagonistic between rich farmers and poor peasants and wage labourers, on issues of tenurial rights, minimum wages and even agricultural prices (since the majority of poor peasants and labourers are net buyers of foodgrains and wages typically lag behind prices), but given their organizational disarray and the numerical preponderance of rich and family farmers taken together, even the leftist parties in India usually follow a multi-class agrarian mobilization strategy in electoral politics, blurring the conflictual issues between farmers and labourers, directing their rhetorical diatribes mainly against industrial monopoly capital in the urban sector and the phantom feudal class in the rural.

Except in localized pockets of North and Central India, the class of landlords which is uninterested in profitable cultivation, but primarily involved in usury and speculation, enjoying the status value of large landed estates and the social power of domination over a retinue of bonded labourers — the class usually described in the Indian literature as 'semifeudal' — has largely disappeared. In most parts of the country agrarian capitalism is sprouting, and in the better irrigated regions it may even be described as thriving. Of course, many of the families of capitalist landlords and rich farmers have also branched out into money-lending, trading, transport, and other business and services. This kind of portfolio diversification has made these families less susceptible to the vagaries of agricultural production, apart from strengthening their urban political and economic connections. Any potential conflict of interests in producer versus mercantile profits (arising, for example, from a government price or procurement policy) is internally managed within the occupationally diversified family or the co-operative society (for agricultural credit, marketing and agro-processing) that these richer families often dominate. In the case of some commerical crops, the interests of rich farmers sometimes clash with those of specialized traders and commission agents, but this conflict belongs more to the arena of agriculture–industry conflicts.

We have talked about the class interests of farmers and their alliance propensities on the basis of those interests. But in the complex hierarchical rural society of India these interests are often overlaid with various kinds of social and cultural divisions. Social anthropologists emphasize the dominance of the diffusing effects of the cross-cutting cleavages of caste and ethnicity, hindering the process of class formation. There is a large, polemical and ethnographically rich literature on this question in India. I shall not go into a discussion of this here, but my own prejudices make me inclined to believe that to take the class interest of the rich farmers as seriously circumscribing the scope and nature of state policy is a meaningful way of approaching the problem, even though caste divisiveness and factional rivalries afflict the articulation and organization of these interests in varying degrees in different parts of the country. In particular, let us consider the *domain* of class interests for our present purposes. When local landlords use their social and economic dominance in a village to effectively frustrate the implementation of a piece of redistributive land-reform legislation, their class interest clearly constrains state action in that localized context, even if their kinship and territorial affinities keep them far from being integrated into any well-organized class in the region or the State as a whole. It has been pointed out that to take all the rich farmers and land-owners as one proprietary class is to ignore the deep political, cultural and economic divisions that make consistent class action virtually impossible even in a localized area: in Uttar Pradesh, Rajput and Jat landowners, even in the same village, are likely to vote on opposite sides; in Bihar the same is true of Bhumihar and Yadav landowners, and more often than not the Bhumihars and Rajputs will strike political alliances with the Chamar poor peasants than with their fellow members of the class of rich farmers. While this is true, for our present purpose it is important to point out that on matters of state policies affecting common class interests of rich farmers, these diverse and often hostile social groups have made common cause: in agitating for higher farm product prices or in frustrating land ceilings legislation, they are usually on the same side even if they may be using different political forums. A major economic issue that divides them does not relate to agriculture or land interests at all: it is their access to jobs in the public bureaucracy where the issue of reservation of jobs for 'backward' castes have excited passions on both sides.

One should also keep in mind that the divisions of caste have different meanings at different levels of aggregation. In a local area the caste of a farmer refers to a *jati*, the relatively small group within which he will find food and marriage transactions acceptable. But in order to cultivate the outside world of politics and bureaucracy and to be effective in channelling the bureaucratic allocation of various subsidies and inputs in their favour, the farmers of one *jati* have to form alliances with other *jatis* of similar occupation, possibly sharing a larger caste group name. These aggregative castes are then more like uneasy political coalitions, held together more by pragmatic class interest than by ascriptive homogeneity: two farmers belonging to the same caste in this larger sense may not accept food from each other, but will pull together for higher prices or lower taxes.

Electoral politics has clearly strengthened these larger caste affiliations. These affiliations and the associated network of patriarchal and patrimonial ties are also useful tools of class hegemony for the rich farmers, who can exercise their economic and cultural domination even without well-knit class organizations and even when they are geographically dispersed. The poor Jat or Maratha peasant gets to share the hegemonic consciousness of his more fortunate kin.

Let us now turn to the third major proprietary class in India: the professionals (both civilian and military), including white-collar workers.[8] It is not customary to include them among proprietary classes, but if physical capital can be the basis of class stratification, so can be human capital in the form of education, skills and technical expertise. We shall show that there can be sufficiently antagonistic conflicts of interests between the professionals, particularly those in the public sector, and owners of private capital, and the usual Marxist practice of submerging them in the petty bourgeoisie and thus treating them as an 'auxiliary class' can be highly misleading. In his 1843 notebook critique of Hegel, Marx describes bureaucracy as just another class (as opposed to Hegel's *allgemeine Stand*) with its own interests; it holds the 'essence of the state . . . in its possession, it is its private property' which is the material basis of its class status. The Anglo-American experience of subordinate bureaucracies, which has shaped some of later Marxist thinking on this question, is sharply at variance with Marx's own experience of the Prussian bureaucracy, which he refers to as 'that omnipotent, all-meddling parasitic body'.

India has a fairly long tradition of powerful bureaucratic functionaries. The patrimonial bureaucrats of Moghal India (such as *fouzdars* or *subadars*) had substantial power, and British rule continued this tradition of a strong civil service.

[8] Here, as in the subsequent pages, I have kept a conceptual distinction between the white-collar workers in the public bureaucracy (which I include among the proprietary classes in civil society) and the political leadership representing the state (sometimes I have referred to it as the 'state elite'). The latter takes the general political decisions which the former are supposed to implement. The process of implementation often generates rental income from disbursement of permits and favours which accrues to the bureaucratic class.

The civil servants were recruited from the traditional literati groups in the population, which, unlike in Europe, had little organic relationship with trade or industry. The expansion in the size of the professional class in the colonial regime was linked more to educational, judicial and administrative developments than to technological or industrial progress. This dominant tradition of an 'independent' civil service, particularly in its upper echelons, with social origins that do not have much of a direct stake in the fortunes of private capital, has continued to this day, even though the proportion of professionals coming from business, farmer or trader families has increased significantly. Except at the lower rungs of the bureaucracy, at the level of local administration, the class origins of officials from families in trade, industry or farming do not directly determine their policy actions.

In a country where the overwhelming majority are illiterates or drop-outs at the primary education level, the educated elite enjoy a high scarcity value for their education and profession. By managing to direct educational investment away from the masses, they have been able to protect their scarcity rent, and by acquiring licence-giving powers at various levels of bureaucracy some of them have increased their capacity to multiply this rental income. It seems the old rentier class in Indian society, deriving its income from absentee landlordism, has now been replaced by the new rentier elements in the privileged bureaucracy, and not infrequently they both belong to similar social status groups and castes. Brahmins and other upper castes are disproportionately represented among the administrators, engineers, educators, and so forth[9] as they were in the old rentier class. For the underprivileged social groups, education offers the quickest route of upward mobility, a passport to the prospect of a secure job in the bureaucracy and the

[9] See, for example, the results of a small sample survey by Taub (1969).

professions. No wonder that some of the bitterest caste struggles in various parts of urban India in recent years have been over the issues of reservation of seats in medical and engineering schools and of jobs in the Government for lower castes.

7

Conflicts in the Dominant Coalition

The three proprietary classes that we have identified — the industrial capitalist class, the rich farmers and the professionals in the public sector — all belong roughly to the top two deciles of the population, and the social and economic gulf between them and the bottom half of the population living in abject poverty is deep indeed. But, as we have already noted, there are significant conflicts of interest among these proprietary classes, contrary to the monolithic image of the 'class enemy' and its co-conspirators that one gets from the demonology of standard radical literature, and we shall try to indicate that these conflicts have serious repercussions on the fortunes of economic growth and of the democratic polity. The size, diversity and the particularly segmented nature of Indian society and economy splinter the forms of articulation of these conflicts, and it is a complex task to trace their manifold refractions in the making and implementation of state policy.

In recent years the conflict that has become particularly sharp and open in public discussion and agitations is that between the urban industrial and professional classes on the one hand and the rural hegemonic class of rich farmers on the other. One of the leaders and ideologues of the latter,

Sharad Joshi of Maharashtra, has described the principal cleavage in Indian politics today as that of Bharat vs. India, the countryside vs. the city, and even borrowing from the rhetoric of the international dependency literature, has pointed attention to what he calls the problem of 'unequal exchange' between India's metropolitan capitalist industrial economy and the vast agricultural periphery of primary producers. The persistent theme in the speeches and writings of Charan Singh, the Jat Prime Minister a few years back, has been on the stranglehold of 'urban lobbies' and the 'parasitic intelligentsia' (his way of describing the professionals). The recent public focus has been on agricultural prices and the 'terms of trade' between the agricultural and the industrial sectors[1] (since the bulk of the marketed surplus of agricultural products is under the control of rich farmers often concentrated in a few States,[2] it is largely the terms of trade faced by them, not by the majority of farmers who do not have much to sell in the market). All the political parties in India have taken up the burning cause of 'remunerative' prices for farm products, although the hard evidence suggests[3] that the administered purchase price has been well above the weighted-average cost of production (including imputed value of farm family labour) since the mid-sixties for wheat and since the mid-seventies for rice, and that over the seventies the Government procurement prices (with 1970–71 as 100) rose to 240 for rice and 170 for wheat by June 1980, while the free-market wholesale prices rose at

[1] In some cases, of course, the conflict has taken the form of direct action, as in the case of sugarcane farmers in Uttar Pradesh lobbying for government take-over of private sugar mills, or the Maharashtra sugarcane farmers' co-operatives acquiring larger and larger shares of the market for processed sugar, outflanking the private mills of North India.

[2] Three States (Punjab, Haryana and Uttar Pradesh) account for 90 per cent of wheat purchases by the Government; four States (Andhra Pradesh, Uttar Pradesh, Punjab and Haryana) for 60 per cent of rice purchases; and two States (Uttar Pradesh and Maharashtra) for most of sugarcane purchases.

[3] See, for example, Subbarao (1982).

lower rates to 207 and 166 respectively. As for the net barter terms of trade between the agricultural and the industrial sector, they do not show much of a trend, taking the last three decades as a whole. There is no statistically significant time trend in, for example, the index of wholesale prices of agricultural relative to manufactured products (presented in Table 12), which may be taken as a very crude proxy of the terms of trade over the period 1950–51 to 1981–82 (a weak − statistically not very significant − decline for the agricultural sector since 1973–74 may be discerned if one uses a dummy variable for the latter period; this possibly indicates the effects of the international rise in the price of petroleum and petro-chemical products like fertilizers). In any case, the net barter terms of trade are not necessarily a good index of changes in the inter-sectoral distribution of income. Studies of inter-sectoral resource flows[4] indicate that through the fifties and the sixties the net resource flows, both on private capital account and on government account, have been from non-agriculture into agriculture and not the other way round; but in the last decade there have been increasing net outflows from agriculture in the form of the financial savings of agricultural households. which reflects partly an expansion of financial institutions into the rural areas and partly a slowdown in investment in physical farm assets. These financial outflows, of course, do not represent unrequited transfers, and in any case, without further information on flows on government account in the last decade, the direction of the overall net flow cannot be determined. Meanwhile the government tax structure remains lopsided in its impact on the non-agricultural sector with relatively insignificant taxation of agricultural income and wealth.[5]

[4] See Mody (1981) and Mody (1983).
[5] Land revenue and agricultural income tax as a proportion of total tax revenues of Central and State Governments declined from 7 per cent in 1951–52 to 5 per cent in 1964–65 to 1 per cent in 1980–81.

Whatever the basis of the grievances, the perceived inequities fuel the conflictual relationship between the rural and urban proprietary classes, and heighten the already existing non-economic tensions arising from cultural and life-style differences between the two classes. These life-style differences, of course, shrink over time as the prospering farmers send some young members of their family to colleges and jobs in towns and as the latter's newly acquired urban values and manufactured consumer goods infiltrate the rural household. It should also be noted that the increased incidence and effectiveness of farmers' agitations in different parts of India in recent years need not be interpreted as an index of increasing economic conflict with the urban classes — more a flexing of the recently acquired political muscles of the rich farmers. The latter have had a strong influence on the formulation and implementation of State Government policies for several decades, but only in recent years has their organizational aggregation at the State and the national level improved considerably, even though their mode of operation and mobilization still remain loose, regionally diffuse and highly factional compared to the 'urban lobbies'. In any case the latter's strength in money power more than matches the former's strength in numbers.[6]

I have pointed to the conflicts of interests between urban and rural proprietary classes. Let me now focus on the conflicts between the professional class in the public sector and the other proprietary classes, particularly in industry and trade. Private capitalists resent the licence-giving powers

[6] Table 19, for example, shows that in 1975–76 while only 5 per cent of rural households had an annual income exceeding Rs 10,000, 17.6 per cent of urban households had such income; in terms of absolute numbers these two groups of rich households (with income exceeding Rs 10,000) were roughly similar in size, 3.8 million in rural India and 3.7 million in urban India. Average per caput income in these two groups of households was, of course, much higher in urban than in rural India.

of (and the attendant delays and waste by) the public professionals who use the popular socialist slogans in consolidating
those powers. Large industrial conglomerates have, of course,
their ways of manoeuvering through the maze of controls
and manipulating it to their advantage in pre-empting competition, but it is costly and can be exasperating. In the name
of helping the 'small man', battalions of bureaucrats wield
the weapons of monopoly control, foreign exchange regulation, industrial licensing and credit and input rationing
to keep the industrialists on the defensive and to increase
their own political leverage and corrupt income. The majority
of businessmen who do not have the clout or the money
power of the conglomerates have to approach these dispensers
or permits and licences essentially as supplicants. The lingering
Brahminical cultural environment that is highly suspicious
of private capital accumulation and often identifies money-
making in trade or industry with greed and dishonesty,
reinforced with modern socialist rhetoric, lends special
legitimacy to the exercise of controls by the bureaucrats
(who, as we have already noted, largely come from the
literati castes). Going beyond controls and regulations, it
is also plain to see that each step in the phenomenal expansion of the public sector, (heralded, no doubt, with a lot of
leftist drum-beating), each dramatic act of state take-over
or nationalization of industry, has been used largely to
expand the job prospects and security of the professionals
and white-collar workers. The same goes for expansion
of jobs in the military hierarchy with the galloping defence
spending since the early sixties. It should also be noted that
the very mode of operation that the regulatory bureaucracy
uses in its dealings with industrialists and traders tends to
divide them and reduce the probability of class-based chal-
lenges to its policy actions. It often deals with members of
the latter group on an individual basis, using selective favours,
granting individualized petitions for exceptions and special

waivers, separating out the Modis, the Swaraj Pauls, the Raunaq Singhs and the like for special treatment, and thereby making it somewhat more difficult for Chambers of Commerce to close their ranks against particular administrative policies.

The bureaucracy impinges somewhat less on the interest of rich farmers, even though in matters of administered prices, procurement, restrictions on grain movements and trade, and distribution of credit and fertilizers, it has numerous powers to exercise and favours to dispense. But the fiat of the bureaucrat, even from the State capital or district headquarters, gets somewhat weaker as it reaches the distant villages where the local rich farmers have things more under their control. The fate[7] of the massive amount of land redistributive legislation in most States — and of the genuine attempts by some well-meaning bureaucrats to implement them — bears ample testimony to the limits of bureaucratic power in the private domain of rich farmers. But even here it is interesting to note occasional cases (as, for example, in Karnataka under Devraj Urs) where civil servants (largely coming from upper-caste families no longer owning much land) effectively formed an alliance with smaller farmers belonging to 'backward castes' to neutralize the rich farmers belonging to dominant middle castes and carry out some redistributive land reforms.

[7] Over the last 36 years less than 0.6 per cent of the total cultivated area has actually been distributed among the landless.

8

The Effects of these Conflicts on Public Mobilization and Management of Capital

We have emphasized the conflicts among the proprietary classes which are sharp enough to distinguish the class alignment in the Indian case from that of most advanced capitalist countries where the dominant class is somewhat more homogenous. No doubt a part of this difference originates in the historical process of weak development of capitalism in India, so that the industrial capitalist class has not yet been strong enough to undermine the economic importance of the class of rich farmers or absorb them in giant capitalist agro-business enterprises; nor has it succeeded in colonizing the bureaucracy and moulding it to suit largely capitalist goals. Besides, the ethnic and regional diversity of Indian society militate against the emergence of a single dominant class whose writ can be enforced throughout the country. Whatever the historical, sociological and structural reasons behind the coexistence of these contending classes, this itself has important implications for the pace and pattern of economic growth. Here we want to link up with our discussion in Chapter 4 on the deceleration of public investment and the rise in capital–output ratio in the public sector as factors significantly associated with the slow economic growth in India. We shall try to put these economic–technological factors in the political context of the class alignments and the constraints they imply on state action.

In spite of an impressive record of resource mobilization largely through indirect taxation[1] and transfer of savings from the household sector through nationalized financial institutions,[2] the bulk of these resources have been frittered away in current expenditures, leaving not enough surplus to finance the massive public investment programmes, particularly in the spheres of coal, transport, power and irrigation, which are clearly needed to boost the rate of economic growth above its current low-level long-run equilibrium. When diverse elements of the loose and uneasy coalition of the dominant proprietary classes pull in different directions and when none of them is individually strong enough to dominate the process of resource allocation, one predictable outcome is the proliferation of subsidies and grants to placate all of them, with the consequent reduction in available surplus for public capital formation. Huge subsidies from the Government budget are required every year to maintain high support prices for farm products, while the vocal urban consumers (as well as the industrialists whose wage costs will go up otherwise) have to be pacified with lower issue-prices of grains at the public distribution points; to maintain low prices of fertilizers, irrigation water, power, diesel, and so forth, for rich farmers; to supply all kinds of underpriced public-sector-produced materials and services for rich industrialists; and to provide substantial subsidies to export interests. The Government is also obliged to supply subsi-

---

[1] In 1981–82 total tax revenues were 16.5 per cent of gross national product (compared to 6.6 per cent in 1950–51) and about 82 per cent of these revenues were from indirect taxation.

[2] Financial saving as a proportion of total (net) household savings went up from 13 per cent in 1950–51 to 39 per cent in 1970–71 to 52 per cent in 1980–81.

61

dized credit through public lending for private agricultural and industrial finance. It is difficult to tally exact totals of all these subsides (both direct and indurect) by the Government each year, but even rough calculations of only the direct subsidies suggest that only three items — food, fertilizer and export subsidies out of the Central budget — taken together exceeded Rs 15 billion in 1980–81, a figure which amounts to half of total gross capital formation in manufacturing in the public sector in that year. The total amount classified as subsidies in the expenditure of all administrative departments of Central and State Governments is estimated to have been about Rs 38.6 billion in 1982–83 (compared to 0.4 billion in 1950–51, 0.9 billion in 1960–61 and 3.4 billion in 1970–71). These subsidies do not include persistent losses in Government-owned irrigation works, State Electricity Boards, Road Transport Corporations and other public enterprises. Nor do they include the vast amounts of subsidies implicit in the overmanning at different levels of public bureaucracy, supporting a whole army of salaried parasites.

The salary demands on the budget, largely from white-collar workers, have grown staggeringly over the last three decades. As a consequence, the gross domestic product (at 1970–71 prices) for public administration and defence multiplied nearly 7 times between 1950–51 and 1980–81, while the total gross domestic product at factor cost multiplied less than 3 times in that period. In the early eighties gross domestic product (at 1970–71 prices) from the public sector in banking, insurance, public administration, defence and other services taken together exceeded the total contribution to gross domestic product from all of registered manufacturing, both in private and public sector, even though at the beginning of the previous decade the latter was substantially above the former. It has also been estimated that since the beginning of the sixties the per caput real earnings of Central Government employees have increased at an annual rate that is two and a half times that of per caput income in the country.

There was a time when it was hoped that the public sector enterprises, after an initial stage, would generate their own surplus for reinvestment. But except for financial enterprises in banking and insurance and petroleum-producing enterprises after the price and output rises in recent years, this hope for the public sector as a whole has remained far from being materialized. By 1981–82, no fewer than 30 public sector units under the Central Government had been recording losses for the previous ten years in a row, and as many as 33 had accumu lated losses that more than wiped out their entire share capital base. In 1981–82, 80 enterprises incurred a loss of more than Rs 8 billion. Thirteen chronically sick units accounted for nearly 80 per cent of the losses; one of the largest among them is the National Textile Corporation, an umbrella company for sick private-sector textile mills taken over by the Government. The enterprises under the State Governments have usually a poorer record. The loss on public irrigation works and multi-purpose river projects for all the States taken together exceeded Rs 4.5 billion in 1981–82. The commerical losses of State Electricity Boards came to about Rs 6 billion in that year; another Rs 2 billion went down in losses for State Road Transport Corporations.

One can, of course, take the position that not all the different kinds of explicit or implicit subsidies or subventions by the Government are wasteful or unproductive from the point of view of economic growth. Subsidized water, power, fertilizers and other intermediate products certainly help in improving productivity. Neither can one judge the social benefits of public sector outputs and services solely in terms of profits and losses, particularly when some of these benefits reach out to the masses. But apart from the fact that there are often cheaper and more efficient ways of delivering the same benefits, what is more relevant to our present discussion is that many of the subsidies disbursed to the rent-seeking proprietary classes did not always help the cause of accumulation and technical change. With all the subsidized inputs and credit to the private corporate sector, the rate of gross fixed capital formation has, if anything, declined in that sector over the last two decades (from 3.0 per cent of gross domestic product at 1970-71 prices in 1961-62 to less than 2 per cent in 1981-82). In the agricultural sector also there is some evidence of a slowdown in private investment in physical farm assets, as we noted in Chapter 2. In some of the States (like Punjab, Haryana, Gujarat and Karnataka) where the rich farmer lobbies are strong and have succeeded in obtaining the major benefits of support prices, subsidies and low taxes on agriculture, the high agricultural growth rates of the sixties have actually decelerated in the seventies and an increasing part of their savings has gone out of the agricultural sector in the form of financial investment.[3] As for the large amounts disbursed as export subsidies, it has often been noted that they are not always reflected in a corresponding rise in net foreign-exchange earnings and are more in the nature of give-aways to prop the profit margins of less efficient units; microlevel data show that there is hardly any positive relation between export performance and subsidies or incentives offered to such units.[4]

Subsidized credit by public lending agencies, of which the last decade has seen a phenomenal expansion, has partly become a big political boondoggle. Lending targets are sometimes set by partisan political priorities,[5] not by con-

[3] See Mody (1983) for some evidence.

[4] See Sen (1982) for some evidence on the basis of the Dagli Committee Report on Controls and Subsidies and the NCAER study of 59 commodities.

[5] It is interesting to recall here Marx's comments in connection with the French Crédit Mobilier in his article in the *New York Daily Tribune*, 21 June 1856:

[The government proposed to convert] all the property and all the industry of France into a personal obligation towards Louis Bonaparte. To steal siderations of maximum social returns. Some of the bigger loan scandals involving the nationalized banks originated essentially in the politicization of public banking, including the packing of banks' boards of directors with people affiliated to the ruling party. In the rural sector there is a dismal record of repayment of loans, primarily by rich farmers, to commercial banks as well as co-operative credit societies. It has been estimated that about half of all demand for recoveries of advances to agriculture by public sector banks has remained overdue for some time. Overdues in the repayment of loans and advances to agriculture by commerical banks were nearly Rs 10 billion in June 1982 (from about 2 billion in June 1976). The overdues of primary agricultural credit societies amounted to about Rs 9 billion in June 1979 (from Rs 3.2 billion in 1970–71). Influential farmers in different parts of the country have made non-repayment of loans from public financial institutions a major plank (along with non-payment of irrigation charges and betterment levies) in the agitations they have led. There have also been reports that in some areas large farmers obtaining subsidized institutional credit have recycled it into their local money-lending operations rather than into productive investment. Concessional financing to the industrial sector has often been used to nurse 'sick' private companies: outstanding bank credit to large sick units alone amounted to about Rs 15 billion by December 1981. Lame-duck private companies often try hard (and pull strings) to get themselves placed on the sick list. In some States such industrial sickness has reached epidemic proportions.

The Indian public economy has thus become an elaborate network of patronage and subsidies. The heterogeneous proprietary classes fight and bargain for their share in the

---

France in order to buy France – this was the great problem the man had to solve, and in this transaction of taking from France what was to be given back to France, not the least important side to him was the percentage to be skimmed off by himself and the Society of December Tenth.

spoils of the system and often strike compromises in the form of 'log-rolling' in the usual fashion of pressure-group politics.[6] The political deal between the contending industrial and agricultural classes in Bismarck's Germany has often been described as the 'marriage of iron and rye'; similar arrangements in southern Europe under the *trasformismo* systems of the last quarter of the nineteenth century have been described as the marriage of cloth and wheat. The dowries of such arranged marriages can be high, and, in any case, since we have identified three major proprietary classes in India, the arrangement here is more like a *ménage à trois* than a marriage, and accordingly somewhat more complicated.

The Indian style of politics is deceptively consensual, but over the years the process of intense bargaining and hard-fought apportionment of benefits among the different partners of the dominant coalition[7] have come out more into the open, and politics has acquired a more unseemly image in the public mind. And, as in all large complicated bargaining counters, there has emerged a group specializing as brokers, who act as agents for different bargaining interest groups, and, of course, take a cut for themselves for services rendered. These are gangs led by a large number of MLAs and MPs, political middlemen who over the years have specialized in the profession of brokerage services. The fees they charge and part of the favours they engineer for their clients in exchange are usually unaccounted in the official statistical book-keeping, contributing to the thriving underworld of

---

[6] In the theoretical literature on public choice, it has long been recognized (see, for example, Tullock (1959)) that majority rule with the trading of votes can lead to too much government spending. For a good survey of the theoretical issues of log-rolling, see Mueller (1979).

[7] We have referred to the loose confederation of the dominant proprietary classes as the 'dominant coalition' for short hand; it should in no way be interpreted as anything more than a tacit and uneasy alliance of convenience among a motley group of interests.

what is called 'black money'. As elections have become more expensive and as their professional expertise in brokerage increased, these fees skimmed off the surplus of the economy have multiplied over the years.

Political democracy has also its way of building up pressures for state subsidies from a growing number of groups even beyond the confines of the dominant coalition. Some sections of unionized workers, small traders and some other small propertied interests, taking advantage of their larger numbers, are increasingly vocal in electoral politics for a larger share of the pie. Regional and sectarian pressures for increased claim to federal money also build up. While from time to time a significant number of crumbs have to be thrown at these clamouring groups banging at the gates just outside the periphery of the dominant coalition, equally expensive is the process of manning and securing those gates, and of controlling the crowds if they every look threatening: the cost of the expanding police and paramilitary forces has risen enormously, particularly over the last two decades (even *per head* of the Indian population, the total expenditure at 1970–71 prices on police including CRP, BSF, CISF, and so forth, rose by 70 per cent between 1960–61 and 1981–82). Thus keeping all the heterogeneous elements of the dominant coalition happy, guarding the fortress, and alternatively coaxing and coercing the intermediate groups banging at the gates all contribute to the mounting non-development expenditure in the budget and leave for the state a dwindling share of the revenues to be reinvested in public capital formation.[8]

Foreign aid, which acted as a convenient cushion up to the mid-sixties, tapered off in subsequent years (until at least the

[8] Krishnamurthy and Saibaba (1983) have estimated that the elasticity of current expenditures with respect to real gross domestic product is 2.1, while the elasticity of real investment is much lower.

beginning of the 1980s), as Table 11 indicates. It is also noteworthy in this context that in contrast to some of the high-growth developing countries which have followed a much more expansionary monetary–fiscal policy and permitted a substantially higher rate of inflation, the Indian state has been by and large *relatively* conservative in matters of inflationary financing of economic growth; over the period 1961–80 the rate of inflation averaged at 8 per cent, a very moderate rate by international standards. The dominant proprietary classes — the rich farmers, industrialists and traders, and even the white-collar workers with partial salary-indexation in the form of 'dearness allowances' — would not have lost much from a more expansionary policy, but the Indian polity is highly inflation-sensitive. With the very low and precarious level of average household income and with the bulk of incomes in the predominant unorganized sector unprotected by any institutionalized indexation, high inflation would tend to shake the roots of the political legitimacy of the rulers. This is an important instance of how the exigencies of electoral politics limit the freedom of manoeuvre of the dominant coalition.

Under these circumstances one of the major dilemmas of Indian development can be simply posed: massive doses of public investment in basic industries and infrastructural facilities and public credit are crucial at the early stages of industrial and agricultural transformation, and yet pressures from heterogenous elements in the dominant coalition for budgetary subsidies fritter away much of the investible public surplus. This is a kind of 'fiscal crisis', in a somewhat different context from that of O'Connor (1973), blocking the necessary accumulation function of the state.

If patronage and subsidies threaten to silt up the channels of surplus mobilization and public investment, the question that comes to mind is why the proprietary classes who have much to gain from economic growth do not pull together in their own long-run collective interest and co-operate in dredging the silted channels. In my judgment this has largely to do with the difficulty of taking collective action in large and heterogeneous coalitions, as Mancur Olson (1982) and others have emphasized in somewhat different contexts. For any single partner in such coalitions, the risks and sacrifices of what may turn out to be a one-sided dismantling of patronage structures carefully cultivated over years may be too costly: the inevitably crowded agenda and the weight of the pre-existing list of complex understandings in large lobbying coalitions make any negotiation on changing the basic rules of the game excruciatingly slow, and the incentives for plodding along the well-worn grooves of short-run rent-seeking are too strong. These general problems are, of course, far more acute in a country of India's size and bewildering criss-cross of interest alignments within the dominant coalition. I have suggested that the partners of this coalition all belong roughly to the top two deciles of the population, but we should remind ourselves that the top two deciles of the Indian population exceed in size the total populations of all but four countries in the world.

The pervading atmosphere of the politics of patronage is also partially reflected in the high capital–output ratio and low capacity utilization in the public sector which, as we have seen in Chapter 4, restrict the output performance even in cases of substantial public investment. Some of these problems are no doubt due to genuine technical reasons or pure managerial inefficiency or lethargy induced by monopoly positions in a sheltered domestic market. But many cases of mismanagement and labour tension may be ultimately traced to the nature of the political regime. Senior appointments in the public sector are sometimes made more on the basis of political patronage than of merit (leading often to low morale in the ranks of the technocracy in the enterprises). Headships of public sector units, particularly under the State

Governments, are indiscriminately used as political sinecures.[9] Efficient managers who fail to satisfy the Minister's political clients are often arbitrarily transferred. Expensive projects are hastily initiated on grounds of political expediency or regional favouritism, without proper design and preliminary spade-work, resulting in long delays and cost escalations. The deliberate promotion of trade unions affiliated to the ruling political party often leads to damaging union rivalries and irresponsible 'economism'. Overstaffing, 'featherbedding', fake payrolls, absenteeism in regular hours and working only for 'overtime' payments, and other irregularities are condoned, if not actively encouraged, by trade unions and their political bosses by citing flagrant cases of corruption, political patronage and cronyism at the top in many public enterprises. Irresponsibilities at the managerial, technical and worker levels thus feed on each other, creating a general atmosphere of demoralization and parasitism on the state. Plundering of public-sector-produced goods by agents of influential politicians in collaboration with public enterprise staff, private contractors and the criminal underworld is far too common. For instance, just between April 1981 and January 1982, 2 million tonnes of coal valued at Rs 300 million were looted from the Asansol-Ranigunj coal-belt alone; percentage losses in transmission and distribution of power under State Electricity Boards attributable to theft alone exceeded 10 per cent for India as a whole in 1981–82, with these percentage losses being much higher for some North Indian States. All this is an indication of how a patron–client regime fostered by a flabby and heterogeneous dominant coalition preoccupied in a spree of anarchical grabbing of public resources

[9] For an example of how extensive this practice is, take the case of the State of Madhya Pradesh. The ruling party had in 1983 a total of 232 MLAs. Of these, 42 were in the State's Council of Ministers, another 74 headed various Government and quasi-official bodies, and about another 100 were said to have been nominated by the Chief Minister to the boards of various public sector corporations.

tends to choke off efficient management and utilization of capital in the public sector.

The evidence of gross mismanagement and inefficiency in many Indian public enterprises acting as a drag on economic growth is often cited by liberals as a justification for their policy prescriptions of de-emphasis on the public sector and of reliance on the market mechanism. The success stories of outward-oriented capitalist growth in some of the developing countries in East Asia (the most dramatic being that of South Korea) are often pointed out as shining examples of this point of view. While there is no doubt that increased exposure to competition and market signals would have induced greater efficiency in resource allocation and management in India, one cannot discuss such policy issues entirely in a political vacuum, ignoring the compulsions of clientelist pork-barrel politics arising from the nature of the polity and its interrelationship with the structures of civil society. Besides, the success story of South Korea, contrary to popular belief, is not one of market liberalism. The Korean state is actively and pervasively interventionist,[10] heavily using the illiberal compliance mechanisms of selective command and administrative discretion, disciplining the private sector primarily through its near-complete control over domestic credit, foreign exchange and underwriting of foreign borrowing. The share of the public sector in value added in the manufacturing sector is quite similar between India and South Korea; there is also little to differentiate the two countries in terms of the control structure over public

[10] For an illuminating account of the structure of state intervention, decision-making and its relationship with private business in South Korea, see Jones and Sakong (1980). Even on the export front their observation is worth noting (p. 98): 'The Korean export spurt is generally attributed to devaluation and export incentives; that is, to getting the prices right. We find surprisingly little evidence for this position'.

enterprises. Yet the all-important difference[11] has been in growth policy implementation, in the speed, flexibility and coherence of government decision-taking in Korea and its ability to translate decisions into action. Far from being a liability on the rest of the economy, the public enterprises have served as the 'leading sector' in Korean growth. In all this, more important than the discipline of the market mechanism has been the ability of the system in the last two decades to largely insulate the framework of economic policy-making and implementation from the clientelist demands of the political process.[12] The single-minded pursuit of growth goals of the Korean leadership has been protected by authoritarian executive dominance, with the legislative and judicial branches of the government being largely irrelevant and the influence of labour unions negligible. Economic targets have been tackled like a military operation, with a tightly focused hierarchical structure of decision-making, untrammelled by the checks and balances of a multi-polar political system.

In general discussions of policy implementation, it is customary to ascribe chronic failures to a lack of 'political will' (whatever that means) or a lack of 'social discipline' (by which Myrdal (1968) characterizes his 'soft' states). In the context of economic growth it is rather the capacity of the system to insulate economic management from political processes of distributive demands, rent-seeking and patronage disbursement that makes the crucial difference. This capacity

[11] I am, of course, ignoring here many other aspects of difference, like the lower extent of price distortions in South Korea, a background of fast growth in its colonial period, a much more educated labour force, successful land reforms, a larger degree of political cohesion resulting from social homogeneity and from a sustained perception of military threat, and so on.

[12] Similarly, in Brazil the role of the insulated parts of the state apparatus, including parastatals like Petrobras and state-controlled banks like BNDE, has been extremely important in the implementation of growth-oriented policies.

does not necessarily depend on the lack of accountability of public sector management: in South Korea there is, if anything, excessive accountability of the public enterprise management to the executive leadership. Nor is the extent of insulation of economic management a monotonic inverse function of the degree of representativeness of government: Japan manages to have a high degree of such insulation with a liberal democratic government (Myrdal's own Sweden is another such example). But in a polyglot and vastly more heterogenous and fragmented society like that of India, this insulation has been difficult to achieve and maintain alongside a pluralist open polity. In the initial years after Independence, the stature and special legitimacy of the Indian leadership allowed it some leeway in this insulation process. But with the increasing plurality of contending interests in the dominant coalition and with the complexity of their mutual interaction often resulting in log-rolling arrangements, the public economy became increasingly exposed. The rapid decline in the importance of what used to be a semi-insulated technocratic institution like the Planning Commission over the last two decades is only one of many symptoms of this process. In recent years the government has occasionally tried to insulate some segments of the bureaucracy (for example, by concentrating power in the Prime Minister's Secretariat), but with its involvement in political gerrymandering, 'fund-raising' and patronage distribution, the latter clearly has not succeeded in getting away from the rough and tumble of day-to-day political wheeling and dealing.

The plurality of proprietary classes (with multiple veto powers) in the dominant coalition in India plays a special role here. In South Korea the government has a close, tightly integrated, working relationship with private business, sometimes crudely described as 'Korea Inc.', with government as the senior partner. This has clear family resemblance to

73

the new forms of 'corporatist' capitalism that have appeared in the high-growth economies of Japan, France, Brazil, and so forth. In the Indian context of contending heterogenous classes, such close liaison and the harmonizing of the interests of the state with big business would have raised an outcry of foul play and strong political resentment, the electoral repercussions of which are not entirely negligible. In recent years, with the relaxation of the industrial policy, the administration in India has attuned itself to the needs and interests of big business a little more than in the past, but the leadership has to keep the latter 'at arm's length' to retain its political legitimacy with the general populace and its peace with the other classes in the dominant coalition. The explicitly relaxed policy that the South Korean government under Park Chung Hee had followed towards increasing business concentration in the hands of the old-style *zaibatsu*-type industrial conglomerates (called *chaebol* in Korea) would have been politically quite costly in India, even though, as we have noted before, the government here as well has diluted many of the provisions of anti-monopoly legislation in recent years. It is this context of a lack of political insulation from conflicting interests, coupled with the strong power base of the white-collar workers in public bureaucracy, that keeps the Indian state, in spite of its pervasive economic presence, largely confined to regulatory functions, avoiding the hard choices and politically unpleasant decisions involved in more active developmental functions.

9

Conflict Management and its Relation to the Democratic Process

In the preceding chapter we emphasized the impact of the heterogeneity of the proprietary classes on economic growth in India. In this final chapter we shall provide some speculative comments on its impact on the nature of the polity, and particularly the democratic process. Marx and Engels often traced the roots of the absolutist regimes of Europe to the matched power of the contending classes in society which boosted the autonomous power of the state. As Engels states in 1884 in *The Origin of Family, Private Property and the State*: 'Periods occur in which the warring classes balance each other so nearly that the state power, as ostensible mediator, acquires for the moment a certain degree of independence of both. Such was the absolute monarchy of the seventeenth and eighteenth centuries, which held the balance between the nobility and the class of burghers.' In the *German Ideology* Marx and Engels have a similar explanation of the persistence of absolutism in the Germany of their time.

While the autonomous power of the state can clearly increase if none of the classes constraining state action dominates the others, the Indian experience suggests that the very nature of class balance and heterogeneity may also make the proprietary classes more interested in tne maintenance of democratic processes. In a country where the elements in the dominant coalition are diverse, and each sufficiently strong to exert pressures and pulls in different directions, political democracy may have a slightly better chance,[1] than in other developing countries, to judge from its rate of infant mortality in the latter in general. This is based not so much on the strength of the liberal value system in its political culture as on the procedural usefulness of democracy as an impersonal (or least arbitrary) rule of negotiation, demand articulation and bargaining within the coalition, and as a device by which one partner may keep the other partners at the bargaining table within some moderate bounds. Even in European history, divisions within the dominant proprietary classes played an important role in the rise of democracy. In France, Louis Napoleon shrewdly used the restoration of universal male suffrage to play the landed classes against the urban; he even reportedly advised the Prussian government in 1861 to introduce universal suffrage since 'in this sytem the conservative rural population can vote down the liberals in the cities'.[2] The cause of liberal democracy in Italy after unification was partly helped by the alliance between the northern industrial bourgeoisie and the southern landed aristocracy. In mid-nineteenth century Britain, competition between the landed class and industrial capital led to significant extensions of franchise. In a related context Marx cites the English proverb, 'when thieves fall out, honest men come by their own'.

In India, such strategic alliances with numerically large

Moore (1966) emphasizes one of the pre-conditions of democracy as a class alliance between the landed upper class and the urban bourgeoisie, which is not dominated by the former.

[2] See Anderson (1972, p. 115).

lower classes or ethnic groups have been quite familiar (the present Prime Minister has successfully used electoral alliances of well-off urban classes with poor tribals and lowest castes in rural areas against some of her rivals with support bases of rich and middle farmers). Populist rhetoric has been a useful weapon in clipping the wings of an over-greedy bargaining partner in the dominant coalition; profuse tears of commiseration with the masses shed on the floor of the Parliament and elsewhere have drowned a rival's extravagant claims. If the industrialists at any time overstep in their bargaining, sure enough there will be an uproar in the Parliament about 'the anti-people conspiracy of the monopoly capitalists'; similar invectives against the 'kulaks' or, somewhat less frequently, against the 'parasitic intelligentsia' will also be aired on appropriate occasions. The competitive politics of democracy thus serves the purpose of keeping rival partners in the coalition on the defensive.

More significantly, the Indian democracy, particularly under the Congress system up until the early seventies, has provided a subtle and resilient mechanism for conflict management and transactional negotiations among the proprietary classes with all their internal divisions and regional and social diversities. The democratic 'machine' of Indian politics,[3] with its well-defined network of distribution of spoils in exchange of support, its highly centralized organization responsive to pressure from important interest groups at different levels in the political system, its institutionalized procedures of transaction which lend it a degree of legitimacy as well as moderation, and its way of absorbing dissent and co-opting leaders of the subordinate classes, has impressed many a political scientist. This machine is vastly more complex and diversified and very much larger in scale than not merely the classical machine model of political clientelism (best

[3] For a similar description of the Congress system, see Manor (1982).

illustrated by the Daley machine in Chicago), but also the Christian Democratic machine in Italy discussed in Graziano (1976) and Eisenstadt and Lemarchand (1981). This complex organization in India was an outgrowth of the multi-class alliance network that Gandhi had forged to fight the British, and as Congress came to power (starting from the levels of municipal and provincial administration in the 1920s and the 1930s), it developed into an elaborate structure of patronage distribution in a multi-class coalition in Independent India. The cause of democracy in India certainly owes a lot to the liberal values of the professional elite at the leadership of the freedom struggle, but its general persistence and the form it has taken has much to do with the political exigencies of bargaining within its heterogeneous dominant coalition. In the nineteenth century history of liberal movements in eastern and southern Europe, one usually notes a long historical gap between the onset of what has been called 'the liberalism of the intellectuals' and the later liberalism of the manufacturers; in India, with a much shorter gap, the proprietary classes have adapted the liberalism of the intellectuals to their own primary needs. So if these classes, for the sake of their own bargaining procedures, if not for anything else, were to remain seriously interested in the maintenance of democratic processes, it would not be very easy for the state to supplant them directly, except at times of military crises (real or contrived).

But over the last decade or so, sizeable cracks and strains have developed in the framework of machine politics that has served the members of the dominant coalition so well for many years. For one thing, democracy has a way of putting ideas in the heads of the lower classes and the proliferating demands for spoils threaten to catch up with the operators of the machine. With sluggish economic growth, which in turn is related to the heterogeneity of the dominant coalition as we have seen, these outside pressures leave for the coalition little room for manoeuvre or not much scope for their selective co-optation tactics, while the banging at the gates gets louder, raising tensions all around. The capitalist democracies of western Europe and North America never faced this problem in comparable intensity (except during the Depression in the thirties), partly on account of the technological dynamism and expansive capacity of capitalism, but also largely because in all these countries the industrial revolution (at least its first round) was completed *before* large-scale democratic demands became pressing.

The fiscal and managerial crises that we have found associated with the pattern of slow economic growth in India have thus in their turn generated tendencies towards a kind of political legitimization crisis. As tensions and frustrations with the old patronage distribution network build up, the legitimacy of the political machine declines, the hegemonic hold of the dominant proprietary classes over the subordinate classes starts slipping away even when their economic grip still remains strong, and some partners in the dominant coalition start looking for other, more secure, ways of conflict resolution, more centralized forms of arbitration. The present Prime Minister, who over the years has shown remarkable skills of political aggregation in a fragmented, continental polity, has, of course, been too eager to provide leadership in this centralized arbitration process. Deeply suspicious of the aspirations of any of the 'bosses' that the machine politics regularly throws up, she used the considerable cunning and state resources at her command to largely wreck this machine, and centralized the whole process of inflows and outflows of spoils and patronage. The once impressive decentralized organization of the Congress Party has largely disintegrated; the principle of popular representation at different organizational levels of the Party has been abandoned; nominated or co-opted political operators and gangsters control much of the political machinery. Forms of liberal institutions, including the independent judiciary, remain, but much of their substantive content is getting eroded. Even the general elections, in which the world's largest electorate participates with an impressive assertiveness, have become essentially occasions for acclamation for one individual leader (as in 1971 and 1980) or her rejection (as in 1977).

In the recent discussion[4] on Latin American authoritarianism, one influential idea has been that of its alleged link with the capital goods phase of industrialization: after the first phase of an import-substituting industrialization oriented towards non-durable consumer goods, the stresses and strains of the 'deepening' of the capital structure are supposed to have facilitated the emergence of what is known as bureaucratic authoritarianism in some of the Latin American countries. A careful analysis of the studies of individual countries, particularly of Brazil and Chile, if not of Argentina, largely shows this link to be weak or fortuitous. In India a substantial capital deepening has taken place in the period when the democratic machine politics of the dominant coalition was in full swing. Here the recent erosion of liberal institutions has less to do with the particular phasing of industrialization, more with the effects of slow growth in cramping the space of political manoeuvre, with the proliferating demands of a pluralist system which makes partners in the dominant coalition jittery, and with the growing sense of insecurity of the political leadership.

The continuing decline in liberal institutions in India has not, however, been accompanied by any corresponding increase in the political insulation of economic managment; if anything, the political emasculation of management autonomy and the privatization of public resources by special-interest groups have become more rampant in recent

---

[4] See O'Donnell (1973) and the subsequent discussion in Collier (1979).

years. The insulation that the leadership has been striving for (in the name of 'national unity' and defence against dark conspiracies inevitably involving 'foreign hands') is more from public scrutiny of abuse of power and from the daily hassles of the horse-trading around the country involved in the elaborate political manipulations conducted from an apex of personalized power structure. The frequently floated balloon of a proposed constitutional change in favour of a presidential system (essentially of the Gaullist variety) is only one indicator of such striving.

Of course, the costs of the personalization and centralization of power are already apparent. When decision-making is personalized or concentrated in a ruling family or a clique in a country of continental dimensions and diversity, the heterogeneous interest groups sometimes find that their access channels to the top are hopelessly clogged and that the royal courtiers and retainers who now act as middlemen are arbitrary in their ways and extortionist in their demands. With the moderating influence of the institutionalized procedures of the old party machine having largely disappeared, the political process has now spawned a new breed of unscrupulous racketeers, undermining the legitimacy of the political system. Political racketeering has also started affecting the management of the public economy, as we have noted in the previous chapter. Excessive centralization, political, administrative and financial, has become a source of corrosive tensions in the federal structure in relation to the States. Within the dominant coalition, big business[5] and urban professionals and the bureaucracy (both civilian and military) will be, in their own interest, committed to a strong centre, but this is not so obvious a goal for the agricultural interests.

[5] It has been noted that even regionally based industrial capital changes its parochial political orientation as its network of operations and markets widens (e.g., the case of the House of T.V.S. Iyenger).

Conflict Management

The latter, regionally diffused and fragmented but increasingly vocal, will be interested in expanding the power of the State Governments which it is easier for them to corner. Attempts by the Centre to rule the State Governments with hand-picked sycophants have backfired, often resulting in intensified faction-fights, intrigues and instability. Without the integrating institution of an effective party organization and without decentralized forms of conflict management, regional frustrations build up, and their outbursts often take the form of sectarian violence and political anomie which undermine the very basis of national unity that centralization is supposed to achieve.

Over the last two decades or so, all over this vast sub-continent, scattered signs of a great deal of ferment and stirring have been discernible. Much of this is still incoherent, unorganized, impulsive and primordial in forms of expression. But people everywhere are now somewhat more aware of their rights and conscious of some of the political and economic issues. The moral and political environment of age-old deference to hierarchical norms is changing, although the glacial pace is much to the exasperation of some impatient observers. In many parts of India the poor have started questioning, with slowly growing assertiveness, what has been one of history's most well-entrenched and ornately elaborate ideological systems of legitimizing inequality and exploitation. This questioning becomes more acute as, with the expansion of the market nexus, the overlords and bosses renege on some of their traditional patronage functions and as, with the periodic exigencies of electoral politics, the vote-mobilizing rhetoric of the competing political notables escalates in radical populism. This turmoil from below in an open polity makes for 'messy' politics, especially when it is added to the pre-existing conflicts among the partners in the dominant coalition that we have emphasized; and this is at a time when the capacity of the political system to manage conflicts, and the institutional modes of compromise and co-optation at intermediate and local power centres, are declining. This had led to dire predictions of the dominant coalition closing its ranks, inducing the state to streamline the administration, to clamp down heavily on the permissive polity, repressing labour unions and disciplining dissent. Others, noting the heterogeneity of the coalition above and the capacity for subtle resistance of those below, doubt if any regime in India can sustain this for a prolonged period, and wonder if, in view of this, it is possible that the dominant coalition may instead find it prudent to make substantial sacrifices in striking downward alliances with some of the subordinate classes and restore the ability of the system to compromise and muddle through. These uncertainties on the political horizon are bound to loom large in any study of the political economy of development in India for quite some time to come.

Appendix
Tables
(1950–51 to 1981–82)

TABLE 1 PERCENTAGE DISTRIBUTION OF POPULATION IN
DIFFERENT EXPENDITURE GROUPS OF HOUSEHOLDS IN
1977-78

Monthly per caput expenditure group (Rs)	Rural	Urban
0.00- 9.99	0.09	0.09
10.00- 19.99	1.29	0.37
20.00- 29.99	8.07	2.49
30.00- 39.99	15.62	7.24
40.00- 49.00	17.60	11.09
50.00- 69.99	26.67	23.90
70.00- 99.99	18.08	24.61
100.00-149.99	8.81	17.44
150.00-199.99	2.25	6.60
200.00 and above	1.51	6.12
Total	100.00	100.00

These estimates are based on National Sample Survey 32nd Round data.

TABLE 2 DAILY STATUS UNEMPLOYMENT RATES IN
DIFFERENT EXPENDITURE GROUPS OF HOUSEHOLDS IN
1977-78

Monthly per caput expenditure group (Rs)	Rural	Urban
0.00- 9.99	14.71	17.60
10.00- 19.99	15.70	26.89
20.00- 29.99	12.35	16.91
30.00- 39.99	9.54	14.23
40.00- 49.00	8.85	13.01
50.00- 69.99	7.05	11.07
70.00- 99.99	6.15	10.10

Monthly per caput expenditure group (Rs)	Rural	Urban
100.00–149.99	5.25	9.18
150.00–199.99	3.53	6.88
200.00 and above	3.95	5.83
All	7.70	10.34

These estimates are based on National Sample Survey 32nd Round data. The daily-status unemployment rate is the ratio of labour days per week reported as unemployed (seeking or available for work) to the total days spent in the labour force (including days unemployed) per week.

TABLE 3   DEATH RATE FOR CHILDREN IN 0-4 AGE GROUP, 1974-76

States	Rural			Urban		
	Male	Female	All	Male	Female	All
Andhra Pradesh	54.8	54.2	54.5	35.3	35.7	35.5
Assam	50.1	48.7	49.4	37.1	29.5	33.2
Gujarat	57.7	61.9	57.8	35.4	38.3	36.8
Haryana	42.8	54.6	48.4	20.0	23.3	21.5
Jammu and Kashmir	33.5	35.1	34.3	13.1	18.1	15.3
Karnataka	33.5	33.3	33.4	15.8	16.9	16.4
Kerala	19.6	20.7	20.1	14.3	14.9	14.6
Madhya Pradesh	63.4	62.7	63.0	30.8	38.0	34.2
Maharashtra	36.2	36.2	36.2	24.5	27.4	25.9
Orissa	51.9	57.5	55.9	30.4	30.4	30.4
Punjab	32.5	41.9	36.8	23.7	28.6	26.0
Rajasthan	61.7	67.3	64.4	26.3	29.4	27.7
Tamil Nadu	48.3	47.9	48.1	29.5	24.8	27.1
Uttar Pradesh	74.0	100.5	86.3	44.5	52.2	48.1

These estimates are based on sample registration scheme data.

TABLE 4   HOUSEHOLD INCOME DISTRIBUTION IN SELECTED DEVELOPING COUNTRIES

Country	Year	Percentage share of household income by quintile groups of households				
		Lowest quintile	Second quintile	Third quintile	Fourth quintile	Highest quintile
India	1975–76	7.0	9.2	13.9	20.5	49.4
Kenya	1974	2.6	6.3	11.5	19.2	60.4
Thailand	1975–76	5.6	9.6	13.9	21.1	49.8
Philippines	1970–71	5.2	9.0	12.8	19.0	54.0
Taiwan	1971	8.7	13.2	16.6	22.3	39.2
Turkey	1973	3.5	8.7	13.3	19.9	54.8
South Korea	1976	5.7	11.2	15.4	22.4	45.3
Brazil	1972	2.0	5.0	9.4	17.0	66.6
Mexico	1977	2.9	7.0	12.0	20.4	57.7
Yugoslavia	1978	6.6	12.1	18.7	23.9	38.7

Source: World Development Reports of the World Bank

TABLE 5 NET DOMESTIC PRODUCT AND SOME COMPONENTS AT 1970-71 PRICES (Rs BILLIONS)

	Net domestic product at factor cost	Agriculture	Manufacturing	Transport, communication and trade	Finance and real estate	Public administration and defence
1950–51	167.98	98.59	16.74	19.53	5.87	4.75
1951–52	171.28	100.13	17.27	20.66	6.07	4.85
1952–53	177.33	105.60	17.67	20.66	6.51	4.89
1953–54	188.82	114.19	18.91	21.45	6.64	5.09
1954–55	193.71	114.17	20.39	22.82	7.02	5.35
1955–56	199.69	113.83	22.02	24.74	7.49	5.52
1956–57	210.71	119.53	23.71	26.30	7.60	5.89
1957–58	206.25	113.21	24.40	26.77	8.13	6.39
1958–59	223.81	126.04	25.34	28.16	8.49	6.82
1959–60	227.68	123.64	26.99	30.23	9.04	7.23
1960–61	243.60	131.43	29.18	32.97	9.25	7.69
1961–62	251.86	132.34	31.76	35.34	10.13	8.18
1962–63	255.83	128.75	34.17	37.52	10.84	9.25
1963–64	269.16	132.04	37.15	40.40	11.63	10.30
1964–65	290.26	144.29	39.92	43.11	12.24	11.42

1965–66	273.35	122.79	40.18	44.12	12.81	11.76
1966–67	275.24	120.84	39.43	45.40	13.35	12.49
1967–68	299.93	140.43	39.93	47.39	13.85	13.01
1968–69	307.78	141.21	41.81	49.80	14.85	13.85
1969–70	326.92	150.34	45.94	52.61	15.68	15.08
1970–71	345.19	163.54	46.19	54.54	16.83	16.35
1971–72	350.28	162.09	47.50	56.06	17.82	17.85
1972–73	345.02	151.18	49.54	57.00	18.56	18.63
1973–74	362.03	162.98	52.52	58.99	18.93	19.80
1974–75	366.24	159.34	54.68	63.12	18.59	20.86
1975–76	401.55	180.66	55.57	68.98	20.25	22.38
1976–77	403.55	168.08	60.40	72.25	22.35	23.70
1977–78	440.45	189.79	64.36	77.46	23.95	25.35
1978–79	464.46	194.50	71.20	83.80	26.26	28.19
1979–80	438.80	167.91	69.91	83.38	26.35	31.46
1980–81	472.35	189.82	70.57	87.34	26.95	35.88
1981–82	496.41	195.77	74.02	93.46	28.48	39.61

Source: National Accounts Statistics

TABLE 6   INDEX NUMBERS OF AGRICULTURAL PRODUCTION (TRIENNIUM ENDING 1969–70 AS 100)

Crop	Weight	1950–51	1960–61	1965–66	1970–71	1975–76	1981–82
Rice	34.0	56.3	88.3	78.1	107.4	124.7	137.1
Wheat	12.2	37.8	60.9	57.6	132.1	159.9	209.7
Coarse cereals	13.9	61.9	87.9	79.3	114.7	111.8	111.1
Pulses	8.1	81.6	112.3	88.0	104.4	115.3	103.7
All foodgrains	68.1	57.1	86.1	75.8	112.9	127.2	140.8
Oilseeds	11.0	66.1	89.8	85.6	116.1	123.8	137.8
Fibre crops	4.0	57.8	96.3	88.5	89.3	103.4	138.4
Plantation crops	2.3	62.7	78.3	91.7	114.8	129.9	161.3
Sugarcane (gur)	7.0	58.1	94.1	105.3	106.4	118.2	153.6
All non-foodgrains	31.9	62.0	88.1	91.3	108.7	119.8	145.9
All crops	100.0	58.5	86.7	80.8	111.5	124.8	142.6

Source: Directorate of Economics and Statistics, Ministry of Agriculture

TABLE 7   STATE-BY-STATE VARIATIONS IN PRODUCTIVITY AND INFRASTRUCTURE (WITH ALL-INDIA AS 100)

States	Index of infra-structural facilities around 1980–81	Index of per caput state income at 1970–71 prices in 1979–80	Index of per hectare yield of foodgrains in 1980–81	Index of per caput value added in the factory sector in 1979–80
Andhra Pradesh	106	98	99	65
Assam	96	81	93	48
Bihar	105	60	89	49
Gujarat	147	129	87	192
Haryana	169	142	139	157
Karnataka	118	109	89	98
Kerala	148	87	138	83
Madhya Pradesh	72	56	60	53
Maharashtra	138	150	60	262
Orissa	94	66	75	53
Punjab	238	200	213	137
Rajasthan	85	75	46	61
Tamil Nadu	168	108	116	139
Uttar Pradesh	113	67	108	40
West Bengal	144	109	118	132

The index of infrastructure facilities as computed by CMIE (1982) is a weighted average on the basis of 3 indicators for power (weight: 20 per cent), 1 indicator for irrigation (20 per cent), 3 indicators for roads (15 per cent), 1 indicator for railways (20 per cent), 2 indicators for post offices (5 per cent), 2 indicators for education (10 per cent), 1 indicator for health (4 per cent) and 3 indicators for banking (6 per cent). The index of per caput State income for Haryana, Kerala and Bihar reported here is computed at current prices (for lack of constant prices data) whereas for the other states it is computed at 1970–71 prices.

TABLE 8 GROWTH RATES IN VALUE ADDED AT 1970–71 PRICES BY INDUSTRY GROUPS

Industry group	Weight in net value added in registered manufacturing in 1978–79 at 1970–71 prices	Annual growth rates in periods		
		1956–57 to 1979–80	1956–57 to 1956–66	1966–67 to 1979–80
Food except beverages	8.16	1.6	2.0	3.7 (a)
Beverages	0.89	7.0	5.1	6.6 (a)
Tobacco	2.16	2.5	3.2	1.5 (a)
Textiles	20.77	2.8	2.3	4.3
Footwear, etc.	0.74	11.5	10.0	14.4 (a)
Wood and cork	0.56	5.0	10.4	5.7
Furniture and fixtures	0.48	6.8	8.9	6.3 (a)
Paper and paper products	2.03	9.2	12.3	7.1
Printing and publishing	1.78	4.4	7.0 (b)	1.8
Leather and fur products	0.28	4.6	2.0	3.1 (a)
Rubber products	1.90	5.1	7.9	4.0
Chemical and chemical products	15.97	9.6	12.6	9.2
Petroleum products	1.66	5.2	–2.9	5.9

Non-metallic mineral products	3.04	4.8	8.7	3.0
Basic metals	9.90	6.1	15.5	5.4
Metal products	2.19	5.0	12.0	2.0
Non-electrical machinery	7.66	9.8	15.9	7.5
Electrical machinery	7.40	11.1	13.1	9.7
Transport equipment	8.30	5.2	7.2	4.6
Miscellaneous	4.13	7.4	10.2	4.2
Total registered manufacturing	100.00	5.3	6.9	5.5
Mining	—	4.2	7.3	2.9
Electricity and gas	—	9.8	9.6	8.7 (a)
Industry	—	5.5	7.1	5.5

(a) denotes statistically not significantly different from the growth rate of the first period; (b) denotes statistically not significantly different from zero.

Source: Ahluwalia, I. (1983)

TABLE 9   IMPORT-AVAILABILITY RATIOS BY INDUSTRY GROUPS

Industry group	Value of imports as percentage of total availability		
	1959-60	*1965-66*	*1978-79*
Food except beverages	4.2	2.9	9.4
Beverages	15.8	7.5	0.9
Tobacco	1.5	0.9	—
Textiles	2.9	1.3	1.6
Footwear, etc.	—	—	—
Wood and cork	22.1	4.5	2.2
Furniture and fixtures	0.9	0.4	0.1
Paper and paper products	23.4	17.1	18.8
Printing and publishing	—	—	—
Leather and fur products	5.4	4.6	0.1
Rubber products	11.5	3.5	5.5
Chemical and chemical products	30.2	17.2	18.2
Petroleum products	43.9	27.8	32.5
Non-metallic mineral products	6.5	2.2	29.3
Basic metals	32.3	22.2	18.9
Metal products	23.4	6.8	6.1
Non-electrical machinery	65.8	56.3	31.4
Electrical machinery	38.1	27.7	9.7
Transport equipment	25.7	15.8	11.6
Miscellaneous	18.8	·15.6	16.4

Source: Ahluwalia, I. (1983)

TABLE 10 SAVING AND INVESTMENT RATIOS (THREE-YEAR MOVING AVERAGES)

	Gross domestic savings as percentage of gross domestic product at current market prices	Gross fixed capital formation as percentage of gross domestic product at 1970–71 market prices	Gross fixed capital formation in the public sector as percentage of gross domestic product at 1970–71 market prices
1951–52	9.5	12.2	3.3
1952–53	9.0	11.1	3.5
1953–54	9.0	10.5	3.7
1954–55	11.2	11.2	4.4
1955–56	12.8	12.8	5.0
1956–57	12.9	14.7	5.8
1957–58	11.8	14.7	5.7
1958–59	11.5	14.2	6.0
1959–60	12.3	13.5	6.2
1960–61	13.1	14.0	6.6
1961–62	13.8	14.5	7.0
1962–63	14.0	15.1	7.3
1963–64	14.2	15.8	7.8
1964–65	14.6	16.8	8.3
1965–66	15.2	17.5	8.4
1966–67	15.3	17.7	7.9
1967–68	14.8	17.3	7.1

TABLE 10 (contd)

	Gross domestic savings as percentage of gross domestic product at current market prices	Gross fixed capital formation as percentage of gross domestic product at 1970–71 market prices	Gross fixed capital formation in the public sector as percentage of gross domestic product at 1970–71 market prices
1968–69	14.8	16.8	6.5
1969–70	15.8	16.3	6.2
1970–71	16.8	16.1	6.2
1971–72	16.8	16.3	6.8
1972–73	17.6	16.7	7.3
1973–74	17.9	16.7	7.2
1974–75	19.2	16.3	6.9
1975–76	20.2	16.8	7.2
1976–77	21.4	17.5	7.9
1977–78	22.8	17.9	8.2
1978–79	22.9	17.7	8.2
1979–80	22.9	17.3	8.1
1980–81	22.8	17.5	8.3
1981–82	22.7	17.4	8.5

These estimates are from national accounts statistics. The data are not adjusted for what are called 'errors and omissions' and net purchase of second-hand physical assets. The 1982–83 figures used for calculating the three-year moving average for 1981–82 are based on 'quick estimates' by the Central Statistical Organization released in 1984. The same price deflator has been used for both public and total gross fixed capital formation.

TABLE 11   COMPOSITION OF SAVINGS (THREE-YEAR MOVING AVERAGES) AS PERCENTAGE OF GROSS DOMESTIC PRODUCT AT CURRENT MARKET PRICES

	Gross savings in the public sector	Gross savings in the private corporate sector	Gross savings in the house household sector	Net inflow of savings from abroad
1951–52	1.9	0.9	6.6	0.4
1952–53	1.7	0.9	6.4	0.5
1953–54	1.4	0.9	7.0	−0.1
1954–55	1.5	1.1	8.6	0.2
1955–56	1.8	1.2	9.8	1.2
1956–57	1.9	1.2	9.9	2.4
1957–58	1.9	1.1	8.8	3.2
1958–59	1.8	1.1	8.6	2.8
1959–60	2.1	1.4	8.8	2.6
1960–61	2.5	1.7	8.9	2.4
1961–62	3.1	2.0	8.7	2.7
1962–63	3.3	2.0	8.7	2.3
1963–64	3.5	1.9	8.8	2.5
1964–65	3.5	1.8	9.3	2.4
1965–66	3.1	1.6	10.5	2.8
1966–67	2.6	1.4	11.2	2.8
1967–68	2.3	1.3	11.1	2.4
1968–69	2.5	1.3	11.0	1.5
1969–70	2.8	1.5	11.5	1.0
1970–71	3.0	1.6	12.3	0.9
1971–72	3.0	1.6	12.2	0.9
1972–73	3.0	1.7	12.9	0.8
1973–74	3.2	1.8	12.8	0.7
1974–75	3.8	1.8	13.6	0.5
1975–76	4.5	1.6	14.0	−0.3
1976–77	4.7	1.4	15.2	−1.1
1977–78	4.8	1.5	16.4	−1.0
1978–79	4.6	1.6	16.6	−0.3
1979–80	4.2	1.7	17.0	0.8
1980–81	4.4	1.9	16.5	1.4
1981–82	4.4	1.9	16.5	1.9

These estimates are from national accounts statistics. The 1982–83 figures used for calculating the three-year moving average for 1981–82 are based on 'quick estimates' by the CSO.

TABLE 12   RELATIVE PRICES, AGRICULTURE TO MANUFACTURED PRODUCTS, INVESTMENT TO NATIONAL INCOME (WITH 1970–71 AS 100)

	Index of wholesale prices of agricultural relative to manufactured products	Index of deflator for gross domestic capital formation to that for gross domestic product at factor cost
1950–51	98.1	78.6
1951–52	92.3	80.8
1952–53	87.1	85.5
1953–54	86.6	86.3
1054–55	80.9	102.5
1955–56	80.3	97.6
1956–57	83.7	92.7
1957–58	84.0	89.3
1958–59	87.6	100.4
1959–60	86.7	99.8
1960–61	82.9	102.0
1961–62	81.8	104.6
1962–63	81.2	103.4
1963–64	81.0	100.9
1964–65	91.8	96.4
1965–66	94.7	93.8

1966–67	98.4	94.9
1967–68	100.3	92.7
1968–69	97.0	95.2
1969–70	103.4	96.9
1970–71	100.0	100.0
1971–72	91.7	100.5
1972–73	90.5	97.4
1973–74	99.8	93.3
1974–75	100.6	99.9
1975–76	91.9	112.4
1976–77	90.5	107.9
1977–78	97.1	106.5
1978–79	95.6	112.1
1979–80	87.6	113.0
1980–81	81.9	120.9
1981–82	87.4	120.7

The series of agricultural and manufactured product prices are from the official wholesale price index numbers (with 1970–71 as the base year) as compiled in Chandhok (1978) and recent reports on *Economic Survey* from the Ministry of Finance. The deflators for gross domestic capital formation and for gross domestic product are from national income accounts.

TABLE 13   STRUCTURE OF INDUSTRIES IN TERMS OF
OWNERSHIP AND ORGANIZATION IN 1978–79

	Percentage in total employment	Percentage in total productive capital	Percentage in total value added
Public sector	26.7	62.1	29.5
Wholly Central government	11.2	24.0	13.0
Wholly State or local government	14.3	36.7	14.8
Central & State or local govt. jointly	1.2	1.4	1.7
Joint sector	5.1	5.8	5.9
Central government & private enterprises	1.5	2.0	2.8
State/local government & private enterprises	3.6	3.8	3.1
Private sector	68.2	32.1	64.6
Corporate	41.3	25.5	52.6
Partnership	21.2	5.9	10.5
Individual proprietorship	5.7	0.7	1.5
Total	100.00	100.00	100.00

This table is based on estimates from Annual Survey of Industries data. One
should keep in mind that this survey does not cover manufacturing outside the
factory sector; the contribution of unregistered manufacturing to total national
income originating in the manufacturing sector is estimated to be about 37 per
cent. The corporate private sector in the table includes co-operatives.

TABLE 14   THE TOP 25 INDUSTRIAL UNITS IN TERMS OF SALES AROUND 1982

Industrial unit	Ownership group	Accounting year ending in	Sales in Rs billions
1 Indian Oil Corp.	Govt	March 1982	80.97
2 Steel Authority of India	Govt	March 1982	29.61
3 Hindusthan Petroleum Corp.	Govt	March 1982	18.84
4 Coal India (combined)	Govt	March 1982	15.49
5 Bharat Petroleum Corp.	Govt	March 1982	15.47
6 Oil and Natural Gas Commission	Govt	March 1982	13.30
7 Bharat Heavy Electricals	Govt	March 1983	11.70P
8 Tata Engineering and Locomotive	Tata	March 1983	8.77
9 Tata Iron and Steel	Tata	March 1983	7.85
10 Madras Refineries	Govt	March 1982	7.74
11 Cochin Refineries	Govt	March 1982	7.69
12 National Textile Corp. (combined)	Govt	March 1982	5.89
13 Indian Tobacco Co.	ITC(F)	March 1982	5.79
14 Hindusthan Lever	Hindusthan Lever (F)	December 1982	5.13
15 Southern Petrochemical Industries Corp.	Joint Sector	(over 18 months)	4.75
16 Indian Petrochemicals Corp.	Govt	March 1983	4.43P
17 Delhi Cloth and General Mills	Shri Ram	June 1982	4.26
18 Reliance Textile Industries	Reliance Textile	December 1982	4.22

TABLE 14 (contd)

Industrial unit	Ownership group	Accounting year ending in	Sales in Rs billions
19 Indian Farmers' Fertilizer Corp.	Co-op.	June 1982	3.62P
20 Associated Cement Cos.	ACC	July 1982	3.57
21 Dunlop India	Dunlop (F)	December 1982	3.41
22 Bharat Earth Movers	Govt	March 1983	3.32P
23 National Fertilizers	Govt	March 1982	3.20
24 Ashok Leyland	Ashok Leyland (F)	December 1982	3.16
25 Indian Iron and Steel	Govt	March 1982	3.05

This is based on data put together by CMIE (1983).
P indicates a provisional estimate.
(F) signifies a primarily foreign-owned company. Only industrial units engaged largely in mining and manufacturing have been covered in this table. Sales figures are inclusive of excise duty. There are problems of comparability of data across companies and of data availability for many closely held companies, which any user of this table should keep in mind.

TABLE 15   SALES OF TOP 20 INDUSTRIAL HOUSES

Industrial house	No. of companies		Sales in Rs billions	
	1972	1981	1972	1981
1 Tata	32	38	6.93	23.90
2 Birla	70	77	5.90	21.62
3 Mafatlal	14	13	1.91	7.98
4 Hindusthan Lever	8	6	1.88	6.10
5 Thapar	35	31	1.55	5.90
6 J.K. Singhania	28	27	1.04	5.52
7 Shri Ram	14	14	1.76	5.31
8 Bangur	44	51	1.43	4.46
9 Kirloskar	15	15	0.71	4.29
10 Modi	9	9	0.94	4.25
11 ICI	7	7	1.49	4.17
12 Sarabhai	11	11	0.96	4.06
13 Mahindra & Mahindra	13	13	0.74	3.45
14 Ashok Leyland	2	2	0.35	3.23
15 Bajaj	29	29	0.83	3.18
16 Reliance Textiles	—	12	—	3.15
17 TVS Iyenger	19	24	0.82	3.09
18 ACC	5	5	0.94	2.70
19 Larsen and Toubro	10	9	0.56	1.80
20 Scindia	3	3	0.51	1.16
Total for these 20 houses			31.25	119.32
Total sales as a percentage of net domestic product in private organized sector at current prices			61	87
Wholesale price index with 1970–71 as base			113.0	270.6

These estimates are based on CMIE (1983). For computing the figures of total sales as a percentage of net domestic product in private organized sector, the figures for the latter have been taken for 1971–72 and 1980–81.

TABLE 16   SIZE DISTRIBUTION OF FACTORIES IN 1978–79

| | *Percentage distribution of* | | |
	Employment	*Productive capital*	*Value added*
I *Employment size range*			
0– 49	14.8	5.6	7.9
50– 99	8.6	3.0	5.2
100– 199	10.1	4.1	6.8
200– 499	12.5	8.3	15.0
500– 999	10.6	10.6	12.7
1000–1999	12.7	14.1	17.1
2000–4999	15.6	12.1	17.7
5000 and above	15.1	42.2	17.6
All	100.0	100.0	100.0
II *Range of gross value of plant and machinery (Rs millions)*			
up to 0.10	14.3	2.2	4.6
0.10–0.25	6.8	1.7	3.0
0.25–0.50	5.3	1.6	2.9
0.50–0.75	3.4	1.0	2.0
0.75–1.00	2.3	1.0	2.0
Subtotal for small-scale sector (i.e., up to Rs 1 million)	32.1	7.5	14.5
1.00–2.50	5.8	2.7	4.2
Above 2.50	59.0	89.6	80.0
Unspecified	3.1	0.2	0.7
All	100.0	100.0	100.0

These estimates are based on Annual Survey of Industries data.

TABLE 17   DISTRIBUTION OF FARM INCOME BY FARM
HOUSEHOLD LAND SIZE CLASSES IN 1975

Farm household land size classes	Rural agricultural population	Area operated	Crop output	Net crop and farm wage income	Livestock income
		Percentage shares in			
Landless	12.3	0.0	0.0	6.2	4.6
Sub-marginal	18.6	3.0	4.2	11.6	9.8
Marginal	15.7	4.0	5.7	11.2	17.4
Small	18.5	12.4	14.9	17.7	19.4
Medium	16.3	19.8	22.0	19.7	21.4
Large	10.7	20.4	20.0	15.4	16.1
Very large	7.9	40.0	33.2	18.2	12.1
All	100.0	100.0	100.0	100.0	100.0

The figures in the table are synthetic estimates based on diverse sources and
assumptions, and should be taken as crude approximations. The farm household
land size classes correspond to NSS household operational holdings categories
of 0.01–0.50 hectares for sub-marginal, 0.51–1.00 hectares for marginal, 1.01–2.01
hectares for small, 2.02–4.04 hectares for medium, 4.05–8.09 hectares for large
and 8.10 hectares or above for very large. The distribution of population across
these land sizes is from NSS 26th Round data; area and crop pattern data by
size classes of farms are from the Agricultural Census. A crucial assumption,
justified as a rough approximation by Ali *et al*. (1981), is that physical yields
for each irrigated or unirrigated crop (as well as labour output ratio for each
crop) is neutral across farm size: the value of output per hectare may, of course,
vary across farm sizes due to differences in crop patterns or irrigation or both.
Similarly, the share of value added in gross output has been assumed to be
uniform across crops (though different for irrigated and unirrigated crops) and
farm size. For other details of computation, see Ali *et al*. (1981).

Source: Ali *et al*. (1981)

TABLE 18 ASSET GROUPWISE PERCENTAGE DISTRIBUTION OF CULTIVATOR HOUSEHOLDS IN RURAL INDIA IN MID-1971

States	Up to 1000	1000–5000	5000–10,000	10,000–20,000	20,000–50,000	50,000+
Andhra Pradesh	8.43	37.27	23.05	16.44	10.68	4.14
Assam	6.63	38.16	25.25	20.78	7.91	1.28
Bihar	7.55	32.79	20.18	18.08	14.96	6.43
Gujarat	1.40	21.63	22.92	26.35	21.15	6.55
Haryana	0.85	4.91	11.65	21.09	34.73	26.77
Jammu & Kashmir	0.41	14.29	26.24	36.63	18.90	3.53
Karnataka	4.56	33.12	23.52	20.52	14.29	3.99
Kerala	9.62	38.25	19.17	16.02	12.33	4.63
Madhya Pradesh	6.25	29.33	25.91	21.54	13.85	3.14
Maharashtra	2.71	26.90	24.35	22.09	17.98	5.96
Orissa	10.23	45.75	23.92	13.53	5.41	1.16
Punjab	0.27	5.99	8.53	12.06	29.17	43.99
Rajasthan	2.53	29.23	26.55	22.95	14.64	4.10
Tamil Nadu	10.31	35.93	22.15	17.83	10.91	2.87
Uttar Pradesh	2.49	24.93	24.58	24.07	18.29	5.62
West Bengal	9.01	37.82	23.24	17.47	10.27	2.18
All-India	5.71	30.95	23.13	20.32	14.72	5.17

Asset groups in Rs

These estimates are from All-India Debt and Investment Survey 1971–72 of the Reserve Bank of India. A cultivator household was defined in this survey as one having an operational holding of 0.005 acre or above.

TABLE 19 DISTRIBUTION OF HOUSEHOLD INCOME BY INCOME SIZE IN 1975-76

Annual income range (Rs 000)	Percentage of households			Percentage share in income		
	Rural	Urban	All-India	Rural	Urban	All-India
1.2 and below	8.3	1.3	6.8	2.0	0.2	1.4
1.2–2.4	29.8	11.6	25.9	13.8	3.0	10.2
2.4–3.6	24.2	18.1	22.9	18.3	7.6	14.7
3.6–4.8	14.6	16.3	15.0	15.4	9.5	13.4
4.8–6.0	9.2	13.8	10.2	12.6	10.4	11.9
6.0–7.5	5.0	10.1	6.1	8.6	9.7	8.9
7.5–10.0	3.9	11.2	5.5	8.7	13.5	10.3
10.0–15.0	3.0	8.6	4.2	9.2	14.6	11.0·
15.0–20.0	1.0–	4.2	1.7	4.5	10.2	6.4
20.0–25.0	0.5	2.1	0.8	2.8	6.6	4.0
25.0–30.0	0.3	1.2	0.5	1.8	4.7	2.7
above 30.0	0.2	1.5	0.5	2.4	10.0	5.0

These estimates are from a household income and disposal survey reported by National Council of Applied Economic Research (1980).

References

Ahluwalia, I. (1983), *Industrial Performance in India: An Analysis of Deceleration in Growth 1956–57 to 1979–80*, manuscript, forthcoming.

Ahluwalia, M.S. (1978), 'Rural Poverty and Agricultural Performance in India', *Journal of Development Studies*, April.

Ahluwalia, M.S. (1984), 'Rural Poverty, Agricultural Production and Prices: A Re-examination', in J.W. Mellor and G.M. Desai (eds) *Agricultural Change and Rural Poverty*, forthcoming.

Alavi, H. (1972), 'The State in Post-Colonial Societies', *New Left Review*, no. 74.

Ali, I., Desai, B.M., Radhakrishna, R., and Vyas, V.S. (1981), 'Indian Agriculture at 2000', *Economic and Political Weekly*, annual number, March.

Anderson, M.S. (1972), *The Ascendancy of Europe, 1815–1914*, Longman, London.

Bardhan, P. (1970), 'On the Minimum Level of Living and the Rural Poor', *Indian Economic Review*, April.

Bardhan, P. (1973), 'On the Incidence of Povery in Rural India in the Sixties', *Economic and Political Weekly*, annual number, February, reprinted with revisions in Bardhan and Strinivasan (1974).

Bardhan, P. (1982), 'Agrarian Class Formation in India', *Journal of Peasant Studies*, October.

Bardhan, P. (1983), 'Regional Variations in the Rural Economy', *Economic and Political Weekly*, 23 July.

Bardhan, P. (1984), *Land, Labour and Rural Poverty: Essays in Devel-*

111

References

opment Economics, Columbia University Press, New York, and Oxford University Press, New Delhi.

Bardhan, P., and Srinivasan, T. N. (eds) (1974), *Poverty and Income Distribution in India*, Statistical Publishing Society, Calcutta.

Bhagwati, J., and Srinivasan, T.N. (1975), *Foreign Trade Regimes and Economic Development: India*, National Bureau of Economic Research, Columbia University Press, New York.

Centre for Monitoring the Indian Economy (CMIE) (1982, 1983), *Basic Statistics Relating to the Indian Economy*, vols I and II.

Chakravarty, S. (1977), 'Reflections on the Growth Process in the Indian Economy', in C. D. Wadhva (ed.) *Some Problems of India's Economic Policy*, Tata McGraw Hill, New Delhi.

Chandhok, H.L. (1978), *Wholesale Price Statistics, India, 1947–78*, vol. I, Economic and Scientific Research Foundation.

Collier, D. (ed.) (1979), *The New Authoritarianism in Latin America*, Princeton University Press, Princeton.

Dandekar, V.M., and Rath, N. (1971), *Poverty in India*, Indian School of Political Economy, Pune.

Dantawala, M. L. (1983), 'Rural Development: Investment without Organization', *Economic and Political Weekly*, 30 April.

Desai, A.V. (1981), 'Factors underlying the Slow Growth of Indian Industry', *Economic and Political Weekly*, annual number, March.

Desai, A.V. (1982), 'Market Structure and Technology: Their Independence in Indian Industry', National Council of Applied Economic Research Working Paper, August.

Desai, A.V. (1983), 'New Forms of International Investment in India', National Council of Applied Economic Research Working Paper, January.

Draper, H. (1977), *Karl Marx's Theory of Revolution*, vol. I, Monthly Review Press, New York.

Eisenstadt, S.N., and Lemarchand, R. (eds) (1981), *Political Clientelism, Patronage and Development*, Sage Publications, Beverly Hills.

Elster, J. (1984), *Karl Marx: A Critical Examination*, Cambridge University Press, Cambridge, forthcoming.

Gouldner, A.W. (1980), *The Two Marxisms*, Seabury Press, New York.

Graziano, L. (1976), 'A Conceputal Framework for the Study of Clientelistic Behaviour', *European Journal of Political Research*, no. 2.

Hazell, P. (1982), 'Instability in Indian Foodgrain Production', research report no. 30, International Food Policy Research Institute, Washington, DC.

Hobsbawm, E. J. (ed.) (1982), *The History of Marxism*, vol. I, Indiana University Press, Bloomington.

Jones, L. P., and Sakong, I. (1980), *Government, Business and Entrepreneurship in Economic Development: The Korean Case*, Harvard University Press, Cambridge

Krishna, R. (1984), 'Stagnant Parameters', *Seminar*, January.

Krishnamurthy, K., and Saibaba, P. (1983), 'Inflation and Growth: A Model for India, 1961–80', Institute of Economic Growth working paper, August.

Manor, J. (1982), 'The Dynamics of Political Integration and Disintegration', in A. J. Wilson and D. Dalton (eds), *The States of South Asia: Problems of National Integration*, University Press of Hawaii, Honolulu.

Mehra, S. (1981), 'Instability in Indian Agriculture in the Context of the New Technology', research report no. 25, International Food Policy Research Institute, Washington, DC.

Miliband, R. (1983), 'State Power and Class Interests', *New Left Review*, no. 138.

Mody, A. (1981), 'Resource Flows between Agriculture and Non-agriculture in India, 1950–1970', *Economic and Political Weekly*, annual number, March.

Mody, A. (1983), 'Rural Resources Generation and Mobilisation', *Economic and Political Weekly*, annual number.

Moore, B. (1966), *The Social Origins of Dictatorship and Democracy: Lord and Peasant in the Making of the Modern World*, Beacon Press, Boston.

Mueller, D. C. (1979), *Public Choice*, Cambridge University Press, Cambridge.

Myrdal, G. (1968), *Asian Drama: An Enquiry into the Poverty of Nations*, Pelican, London.

Nayyar, D. (1978), 'Industrial Development in India: Some Reflections on Growth and Stagnation', *Economic and Political Weekly*, special number, August.

National Council of Applied Economic Research (1980), *Household Income and its Disposition*, New Delhi.

References

O'Connor, J. (1973), *The Fiscal Crisis of the State*, St Martin's Press, New York.

O'Donnell, G. A. (1973), *Modernization and Bureaucratic-Authoritarianism: Studies in South American Politics*, Institute of International Studies, Berkeley.

Olson, M. (1982), *The Rise and Decline of Nations: Economic Growth, Stagflation and Social Rigidities*, Yale University Press, New Haven.

Planning Commission, Government of India (1977), *Studies on the Structure of Indian Economy and Planning for Development*, New Delhi.

Poulantzas, N. (1983), *Political Power and Social Classes*, New Left Books, London.

Report of the Working Group on Savings (1982), *Capital Formation and Saving in India*, Bombay.

Raj, K. N. (1976), 'Growth and Stagnation in Indian Industrial Development', *Economic and Political Weekly*, 26 November.

Rakshit, M. K. (1982), 'Income, Saving and Capital Formation in India: A Step Towards a Solution of the Saving-Investment Puzzle', *Economic and Political Weekly*, annual number.

Rangarajan, C. (1982a), 'Agricultural Growth and Industrial Performance in India', research report no. 33, International Food Policy Research Institute, Washington, DC.

Rangarajan, C. (1982b), 'Industrial Growth: Another Look', *Economic and Political Weekly*, annual number.

Sarma, J. S., and Roy, S. (1979), 'Two Analyses of Indian Foodgrain Production and Consumption Data', research report no. 12, International Food Policy Research Institute, Washington, DC.

Sen, A. K. (1974), 'Poverty, Inequality and Unemployment: Some Conceptual Issues in Measurement', in Bardhan and Srinivasan (1974).

Sen, S. (1982), 'From Import Substitution to Export Promotion: Policy Planning in India's Foreign Trade Sector', *Economic and Political Weekly*, annual number, April.

Shetty, S. L. (1978), 'Structural Retrogression in the Indian Economy since the Mid-Sixties', *Economic and Political Weekly*, annual number, Februrary.

Skocpol, T. (1982), 'Bringing the State Back In', *Items*, Social Science Research Council, New York, nos 1/2.

Srinivasan, T. N., and Narayana, N. S. S. (1977), 'Economic Performance since the Third Plan and its Implications for Policy', *Economic and Political Weekly*, annual number, February.

Stepan, A. (1978), *The State and Society: Peru in Comparative Perspective*, Princeton University Press, Princeton.

Subbarao, K. (1982), 'Food Production, Prices and Income Distribution: A Review of Recent Trends in India', manuscript.

Sukhatme, P. V. (1978), 'Assessment of Adequacy of Diets of Different Income Levels', *Economic and Political Weekly*, special number, August.

Taub, R. (1969), *Bureaucrats Under Stress*, University of California Press, Berkeley.

Taylor, L. (1983), *Structuralist Macroeconomics*, Basic Books, New York.

Trimberger, E.K. (1978), *Revolution from Above: Military Bureaucrats and Development in Japan, Turkey, Egypt and Peru*, Transaction Books, New Brunswick.

Tullock, G. (1959), 'Some Problems of Majority Voting', *Journal of Political Economy*, December.

Vaidyanathan, A. (1977), 'Constraints on Growth and Policy Options', *Economic and Political Weekly*, 17 September.

World Bank (1983a), *China: Socialist Economic Development*, vol. I, Washington, DC.

World Bank (1983b), *World Development Report*, Washington, DC.

Epilogue
on the
Political Economy
of Reform in India

Epilogue
The Political Economy of Reform in India

'The reformer has enemies in all those who profit by the old order, and only lukewarm defenders in all those who would profit by the new.'

– Niccolo Machiavelli, in *The Prince* (1513), Ch. VI.

I

In the last few years I have often been asked if my thinking on the low-level equilibrium described in the main part of this book (written nearly 15 years ago) have changed in view of the on-going economic reforms. Starting in the mid-1980s, but accelerating since the external payments crisis in mid-1991, India's industrial licensing and regulatory policies, trade, tax, investment, and fiscal policies have undergone substantial changes. In this epilogue I shall briefly discuss the political economy of reform in India. I shall comment less on what should or should not have been done, and more on the socio-political background of what has been done: less on what is desirable and more on what is feasible. In doing this I shall have to necessarily move beyond economics, and at times dabble in political sociology. My comments are also confined to broad long- or medium-run patterns, and not to the ups and downs of the economy in the short run.

I have noticed in recent literature two opposed general positions on the pace and prospect of reforms. One of these takes the rosy view that dramatic changes in policy have taken place since 1991, and that more could be done but for the messy politics that occasionally slow down reforms; for example, those relating to the insurance sector or industrial labour; but the reform process is now essentially irreversible, and most political leaders give assurances to this effect to business, despite rhetorical deviations in some of their public speeches. The other view is more pessimistic: only the easier reforms have been handled so far (given that the nightmarish extent to which the system of licenses and permits was stretched in the earlier regime was unacceptable to most people) while many difficult reforms have been stalled and are likely to remain so, given the path of rag-tag coalition politics that the country seems to be inevitably taking.

My own position in this respect is somewhere in between these two opposed general views. But I would like to differentiate my view from another intermediate position, taken, for example, by Jenkins (1997). This position is essentially about reform by stealth: that a great deal of substantial reforms has been accomplished, avoiding major headlines or political confrontations; a process of slow but steady creeping reform has set in, according to this view, and is likely to continue. In my judgment this intermediate position has considerable plausibility. I shall therefore discuss this position at some length, and point out where I agree and where I don't.

But first we need to work at some aggregative statistics on growth and investment, to give us some indication about the quantum of these changes in terms of macroeconomic outcome. Next we shall discuss some methodological points to help us interpret this data. Finally we will move into issues concerning political-economy.

For the macro data we shall draw upon the careful analysis of the National Accounts Statistics for the period of 1980–81 to 1995–96 made by Nagaraj (1997). One advantage of these statistics is that they allow for a relatively long time-series, and one does not have to depend on simple year-to-year variations in growth rates. On the basis of the time series one can say that over-all GDP, as well as sectoral GDP in primary and tertiary sectors, roughly maintained its earlier (i.e. of the 1980s) growth rates in the 1990s. There have been no dramatic changes in these rates. In fact there is a small but statistically significant decline in the secondary sector (including manufacturing) in the 1990s compared to the 1980s (the addition of the last two years, 1996–97 and 1997–98, when data are available, is unlikely to change this as on all indications the growth rates in the industrial sector have slowed down in these two years).

Within the manufacturing sector one expects some decline in import-substitute industries with trade liberalization.[1] This has happened sharply in the capital goods industries. One indicator of the increased competition in these industries is the fall in prices of machinery and equipment relative to the GDP deflator since the late 1980s. Some consumer goods, particularly durables, experienced growth, fueled by a rise in effective protection (due to devaluation as well as a fall in the relative price of inputs). Contrary to the usual expectation of the effect of trade liberalization, there has, however, not been much of an increase in the growth of traded, labour-intensive goods. In fact the growth rate in the unregistered manufacturing sector (which employs nearly half the total labour in manufacturing) declined from an average of 7.6 per cent in 1986–91 to 5.7 per cent in 1992–96. There has also been a marked decline in the growth rate of total employment

---

[1] On the other hand, with imperfect competition trade liberalization may increase the perceived elasticity of demand facing each firm, lower its mark-up, and increase output. The domestic market for Indian firms is, however, often regionally segmented, reducing the impact of national-level competition.

Epilogue on the Political Economy of Reform in India

in the organized sector as a whole in the 1990s as compared to
the 1980s. Again, contrary to expectation, some of the non-traded,
tertiary sectors recorded a significant increase in growth. Much
of the large rise in the growth rate in private corporate gross fixed
capital formation has gone into the tertiary sector (most likely into
finance and real estate). The share of infrastructure in total gross
fixed capital formation in the economy declined from 37 per cent
in 1986–87 to 26 per cent in 1995–96. This was associated with
the decline in the public sector gross capital formation as a
percentage of GDP.[2] It is now agreed on all counts that India's
creaking infrastructure (power, railways, roads, ports, etc.) is the
major bottleneck on industrial growth.

In interpreting the decline in the manufacturing growth rate in
the 1990s it is important to keep in mind one methodological
point: the effects of liberalization should be carefully distinguished
from those of macroeconomic stabilization. Some of the adverse
effects of the credit crunch in the first half of the 1990s or the fiscal
squeeze necessitated by the past and present profligacy in our
public fisc should not be attributed to liberalization *per se*, even
in cases where one could think of better ways of carrying out the
corrective fiscal and financial policies. For example, the sharp
decline in growth of the unregistered manufacturing sector noted
above may have much to do with the difficulty of getting credit
that this sector faced.[3] It is also to be noted that the growth rate
in the 1980s, financed to some extent by large external borrowings, may not have been macroeconomically sustainable for long,
and thus any comparison with the eighties growth rate has to be
qualified to that extent. It is also possible that it is as yet too soon

[2] Capital expenditure of the Central and State Governments taken together as
a proportion of GDP declined from 8.3 per cent in 1990–91 to 5.7 per cent in
1995–96.

[3] A Report of Internal Group on Small Scale Industries in the Planning
Commission in 1997 observes that capacity utilization in this sector is only around
50 per cent, and one of the main factors responsible for this underutilization is the
inadequacy of credit.

122

for the effects of the structural changes that have taken place since 1991 to show up in aggregative growth statistics. In scattered parts of the economy (including in some public enterprises)[4] increased competition and restructuring may have improved total factor productivity, but hard evidence for this on a sustained basis and an adequately large scale is not yet available.

The other methodological point to note in discussing the effects of policy changes is that some reforms came not by design but more as unintended consequences of bankruptcy. This is particularly the case at the State level. Some reforms have generated a chain reaction creating a demand for pushing the reforms further than what was originally intended. We shall come back to this point when we discuss the issue of creeping reforms.

II

Next we discuss the politics of reforms. Politics is about distributive conflicts, about winners and losers, and how they get organized about it or fail to. Who are the losers from reforms so far? The most vocal group in opposition is organized labour. Of course, not many jobs have been lost in government service (the part of the Fifth Pay Commission Report which recommended streamlining and reducing the future size of the government did not have any takers, in contrast to the part about pay revisions), although there is a fear of potential job loss from privatization. In contrast to the white-collar labour unions, the labour movement for the manual or blue-collar workers is actually highly fragmented, an issue we shall take up later. The other vocal group, ignoring the occasional vandalism against Kentucky Fried Chicken or Cargill Seed Farm by organized farmers, is that of Indian business houses. Some of them have been clamouring for a 'level

[4] Nagaraj (1997) refers to the significant rise in profitability (gross profit as percentage of capital employed) of central government public sector enterprises in the 1990s in general, and in the plant load factor of thermal power plants in particular.

123

playing field', when they perceived their traditional family control to be threatened by foreign multinationals.[5] Patriotism is, of course, the first refuge of laggards in competition.[6] Yet all major political parties (the Left parties, BJP, the Janata Party and even the Congress) have played the 'swadeshi' tune on this issue at election time.

The actual, as opposed to potential, losers in the 1990s may have been many small-scale enterprises. They were hit hard by the credit crunch, which was part of the macro stabilization policy. It may, of course, be claimed that even within the broad framework of stabilization some government policies, for example, those inducing transfer of savings to the equity markets, may have made access to finance more difficult for small enterprises compared to large companies. With the freeing of bank lending rates and the fiscal concessions for deductibility of interest costs that the corporate sector enjoys, the interest-rate structure has become more regressive, to the disadvantage of the unorganized sector.

In general there has not been much political backlash against reforms and no serious pitched battles (as opposed to occasional rhetorical skirmishes) have been fought on the issue of liberalization. Many State-level political leaders, irrespective of which party they belong to, have supported liberalization. If not for any other reason, simply because it has been associated with a more open-door policy for foreign investment, providing a way out of fiscal bankruptcy. The lack of serious opposition to reforms has

[5] The threat as yet is largely exaggerated for the corporate sector as a whole—a comparison of the *Business India* 100 in 1995 with the listing in 1978 suggests that the predominance of Indian business houses remains about the same. This is particularly the case in asset holdings. Foreign firms' share in fixed asset formation in the corporate sector remains at about 10 per cent in the 1990s, as can be seen from estimates of the Centre for Monitoring the Indian Economy (CMIE).

[6] For example, a company like Bajaj (whose chairman has been one of the most vocal in demanding restrictions on foreign investment) has been losing market share largely because it does not use its own R&D, while its competitors have their own design and development units.

sometimes been interpreted as evidence of lack of substantive reforms, because reforms are not supposed to be painless. This view is not quite correct. A more plausible view, as exposited, for example, by Jenkins (1997), is that there has been a great deal of piecemeal reform through a political process of diffusing resistance on part of the vested interests in various ways, without causing massive political confrontations. Like the stealth bomber, reform in India has largely avoided the political radar screen.

This process of diffusion of resistance may be illustrated by referring to the three major forms it has taken. Firstly, while some large business houses have lost on account of increased competition from new (often medium-sized) business groups particularly at the regional level (providing a new constituency of reforms)[7], the former have gained elsewhere as restrictions to entry in some sectors (earlier reserved only for public enterprises) have been eased. Thus, the potential opposition from large business houses has been muffled. Secondly, there has been a diffusion of resistance through regional fragmentation. As power has shifted more to the regions (indicated not just by the prominence of regional parties in power-brokering, but also by the increasing effective autonomy of the regional wings of national parties from the directives of the central party leadership), some regional governments, backed as they increasingly are by regional capital, have looked the other way when pre-existing restrictive rules have been breached or not effectively enforced. The opposition to non-implementation of existing laws has thus been splintered. This has happened, for example, in the case of opposition by labour unions to lockouts by owners of industrial firms or the non-enforcement of Section 25 of the Industrial Disputes Act, under which government permission is needed to sack workers. These are instances of a kind of reform by default.

Third is the case of reform by stealth or creeping reforms, as in the case of a slow chipping away at restrictions without causing

[7] In any case the regional business groups knew that the major beneficiaries of the old licensing system were the national big business houses.

much of a political splash. For example, in December 1997 the asset limit for small industries was multiplied five-fold (from Rs 6 million to Rs 30 million in terms of the value of plant and machinery), even though the number of products exclusively reserved for these small industries has not declined very much. Similarly, in some States the rules for acquisition and conversion of land for private industrial projects were allowed to be manipulated (evading the restricitive urban land-ceiling laws), in the process generating a great deal of illicit income for politicians and promoters. The monopoly power of large public sector companies has been chipped away by backdoor privatization on a small scale or by allowing industrial firms to have captive power plants or coal mines (or allowing them to import if the domestic public enterprise fails in its supply commitments).

Reform by stealth has been especially important in the case of labour laws. These laws, particularly those relating to job security and automatic promotion, are on paper among the most stringent in the world. Several attempts to change these laws have faced enormous opposition, difficulty and delay much to the despair of reformers. Yet in practice, employers have often got away with many changes:

(i) many workers have been pushed out under the so-called voluntary retirement scheme with or without legal compensation, and few have been retrained or redeployed;

(ii) there has been widespread use of contract or casual labour, substituting for regular employees, sometimes through job or task redefinition;

(iii) many unviable units have actually been closed through various subterfuges (in fact the average number of days lost due to lockouts now far exceeds those due to strikes);

(iv) there have been many cases of sub-contracting work out to small-scale units or backward areas, where the enforcement of the existing laws is also backward.

While there are large elements of truth in the position thus taken by Jenkins (1997) and others, I happen to disagree with this position on some major points. Diffusion of resistance through regional fragmentation is limited on important issues of restructuring at the national policy level, where vested interests are nationally organized. For example, in the case of restructuring the management of large public enterprises at the centre and giving them *real* autonomy (not just the 'smoke and mirrors' of MOUs in the past or the 'navaratna' or 'mini-navaratna' status proposed currently); or in breaking the unholy nexus between the public-enterprises hierarchy, their private clients and the criminal underworld and their political patrons; or in restructuring the insurance sector, or in the internal organization of public financial institutions;[8] or in reducing family control over large private-sector enterprises. Similarly, the practice of looking the other way while labour laws get diluted, may not be enough to attract foreign investors who may insist on more tangible guarantees. In general, reforms, if they remain clandestine, may strain credibility in the medium and long run.

The staggering burden of government subsidies, placating various powerful interest groups, shows how may crucial political-economy issues remain unresolved. A detailed study by the National Institute of Public Finance and Policy, reported in Srivastava and Sen (1997), provides a fairly comprehensive estimate of the explicit and implicit budget-based subsidies.[9]

[8] There have, however, been significant, though slow and halting, financial sector reforms. These include the deregulation of interest rates, more competition in the financial sector, insistence on capital adequacy norms in most public sector banks, etc. The 'non-performing assets' as a proportion of their total advances have now been brought down to below 20 per cent.

[9] This includes, apart from explicit cash subsidies (e.g. on food, fertilizer and export), interest or credit subsidies (i.e. loans given at below market rates), tax subsidies (e.g. tax exemption of medical expenses, deduction of mortgage interest payment from taxable income, etc.), in-kind subsidies (e.g. provision of free medical services), equity subsidies (investment in equity in State enterprises yielding low dividends), procurement subsidies (say in government purchase of foodgrains), and regulatory subsidies (administered pricing). The estimate, by its method of computation, includes the effects of cost overruns, wastages and inefficiencies on capital projects, and thus goes beyond the usual meaning of subsidies.

Accordingly to this estimate the budget-based[10] subsidies of the Central and State Governments taken together amounted to about Rs 1.4 trillion, which is 14 4 per cent of GDP (or about twice the size of the aggregate fiscal deficit) in 1994–95. This study computes subsidies as the excess of providing a service over the recoveries from that service (excluding defence and general administration). If one also excludes expenditure items like primary education, public health and sanitation, flood control and drainage, roads and bridges, soil and water conservation, agricultural and various scientific research, and many social welfare schemes, and concentrates on what the study (not quite accurately) calls 'non-merit goods and services' (a large part of which go to the non-poor), the total estimate of such subsidies alone amounts to Rs 1.04 trillion, or 10.9 per cent of GDP in 1994–95.

Then there is the colossal public debt, servicing which takes up a large and increasing part of budgetary funds, moving inexorably towards an internal debt trap, and keeps the interest rates high, choking private investment.[11] The interest payments of the Central Government on the public debt as a proportion of GDP rose from about 3 per cent in the mid 1980s to 4 per cent in 1990–91, and then to about 5 per cent in the mid 1990s. While the fiscal deficit of the consolidated public sector (including the Central and State Governments and non-financial public enterprises) as a proportion of GDP declined slightly from about 12 per cent in 1990–91 to about 10 per cent in 1995–96. A large part of this was the revenue deficit (used primarily for government consumption), which as a proportion of GDP does not show any decline. This deficit steadily increased over the 1980s, and then

[10] This estimate excludes an off-budget subsidy like petroleum subsidy, which in 1994–95 was about Rs 66 billion (by 1997 the 'oil pool deficit' climbed to more than three times that amount).

[11] Recently the finance ministry had a formal agreement with the Reserve Bank giving the latter a great deal of autonomy in the matter of monetization of the public debt. This illustrates that the Indian state is more sensitive to the short-run political dangers of inflation than to the long-run costs of choking investment.

after a decline in the first two years of 'adjustment' (1991–93) went up significantly. It is likely to go up again after the hefty upward revision of wage and salary scales of government employees at all levels. This revision is to be shortly implemented following upon (and exceeding) the recommendations of the Fifth Pay Commission (and its usual chain reactions for other public services at the Central and State levels); at the mere hint of a strike by the Central Government employees, the Government capitulated.

The budgetary problems are severe, particularly at the State level, where the governments, exposed as they are more closely to some of the particularistic interest groups, are practically bankrupt in many cases.[12] The revenue deficit of the States has trebled over the 1990s so far. In some cases 'development grants' for capital projects authorized by the Planning Commission are being used by the States largely to pay salaries to public officials. An increasingly larger share of the Central loan to the States is utilized to repay earlier loans and the States' aggregate outstanding loans to the Centre was nearly Rs 1.5 trillion by the end of the financial year 1996–97. Circumventing the constitutional ceiling on market borrowings by State governments, the State-owned enterprises are issuing bonds with State government guarantees (generating large contingent liabilities) whose outstanding level nearly quadrupled over the first half of the 1990s.

And yet a chief minister celebrated his recent election victory by announcing that the farmers, a large and powerful lobby in his State, do not have to pay for irrigation water or electricity. In many other States as well, water and electricity are provided at throw-away prices (as are higher education and urban transport), much below even the operational and maintenance costs of the facilities, not to speak of the capital cost. In 1994–95 the gross electricity subsidy of all States for the agricultural sector alone

---

[12] In Uttar Pradesh, for example, debt servicing is now more than the tax revenue of the State.

exceeded Rs 100 billion. In 1996–97 the annual commercial losses (excluding subsidies) of the State Electricity Boards were more than six times what they were in 1985–86, and their combined rate of return is now estimated to be a negative 16.5 per cent.

There is a growing sense, in some quarters, that bankruptcy and the diminishing transfers from the Centre[13] will eventually make the States awaken to the hard reality and the pressing need for reform. Attempts are afoot, for example, to restructure the operations of the State Electricity Boards in a few States (like Orissa and Andhra Pradesh). As States are increasingly asked to fend for themselves and as inter-State competition to lure private investment heats up, this game is clearly to the advantage of the infrastructurally already better-off States. What is less, clear, however, is how the Indian federal system will resolve the tension between the demands of the better-off States for more competition, and those of other States (which a weaker Centre can ill afford to ignore politically) for redistributive transfers through constitutional bodies like the Finance Commission or extra-constitutional agencies like the Planning Commission. Can, for example, a shaky coalition government at the Centre, dependent on MPs from infrastructurally weak States like Bihar, Uttar Pradesh or Madhya Pradesh, ignore their redistributive demands to compensate them for losing out in the inter-State competition for private investment? Such bail-outs are likely to give wrong incentives in resource mobilization efforts by these States.

On the whole one should not exaggerate the extent of shift in the basic political equilibrium inspite of all the impressive changes that have taken place in economic policy. About fifteen years ago when I wrote the main part of this book, I had described a system of political gridlock in India, originating in the collective

---

[13] The total net transfers from the Central to the State Governments, (i.e. the States' share of Central taxes, and loans and grants to the States less interest and amortization of loans) fell from more than 6 per cent of GDP in 1990–91 to 4.7 per cent in 1995–96.

action problems of a large, heterogenous coalition of dominant interest groups with multiple veto powers, and with no interest group powerful enough to hijack the State by itself; the system thus settled for short-run particularistic compromises in the form of sharing the spoils through an elaborate network of subsidies and patronage distribution, to the detriment of long-run investment and economic growth. Since then there has certainly been an increase in the diversity, fluidity, and fragmentation in the coalition of dominant interest groups. The industrial scene is less dominated today by a few big business houses, with the rise of medium-sized and regional business groups (particularly in textiles, sugar, cement, steel, chemicals and fertilizers in western and southern India) providing competition and conflict.[14] The rich farmer families are diversifying their investments and often branching out into private trade and commerce, real estate, transport, and small industry (particularly in sugar and rice mills, food processing, etc.), and as such are not averse to expansion of opportunities and easing of government regulations in the urban sector. There is also a discernible change in the mindset of large sections of the elite regarding the limits of the role of the State.

There is a slow, and at times grudging, acceptance within the bureaucracy that the Indian State has overextended itself in the economy, far beyond the limits of its administrative capacity. Some of the new entrepreneurs, belonging as they do to the families of senior bureaucrats, army officers and other members of the professional classes or sharing ties through education in elite engineering and business schools, have forged new links between the bureaucracy and private capital. Regional governments have much stronger links with regional capital now. Furthermore, most members of the dominant coalition, families

[14] The composition of the list of top 20 business houses has changed substantially in the last 25 years, with the entry of many new business houses and the exit of some old ones. Some of the regional business groups are now quite influential in business lobbies like CII at the national level.

131

in the industrial and professional classes in particular but also some rich farmer and trader families, have now some close or distant relatives among non-resident Indians; a larger interaction and communication with foreign countries has helped thaw some of the antiquated, hard, autarchic attitudes. Meanwhile, the ideological props for pervasiveness of State control and regulations that the left intellectual community used to provide have been crumbling with the precipitous decline of State socialism in different parts of the world.

All these changes and realignments in the composition and attitudes of the dominant coalition have made some of the deregulatory reforms more acceptable than before. But, as we have mentioned in the preceding paragrasp, one should not underestimate the enormity and tenacity of vested interests in the preservation of the old political equilibrium of subsidies and patronage distribution. Matters are further complicated by the evolving democratic forces, unleashed in an extremely hierarchical and heterogenous society. This political sociology of reforms and its implications are discussed in the next section.

III

Along with political power drifting from the Centre to the regions, there is an associated drift towards the backward and lower castes. This is clearly a sign of democratic progress in an unequal society. The numerical strength and increased assertiveness of some of the historically subordinate groups have compelled the upper classes and castes to form downward alliances and brought to the fore political actors from backward communities and regions. These players may be uninitiated in the etiquette of parliamentary democracy and in the social graces of modernity, but are quite astute in pursuing the interests of their constituencies (and, of course, their own self-interest). This victorious march of democracy in India with all its banality and gaudiness would have impressed Alexis de Tocqueville (1835) who had described the

turmoil in nineteenth century Europe generated by rising democratic aspirations in a highly unequal society.

What is disturbing, however, is that the diminishing hold of elite
control and the unfolding of populist democracy to reach the lower
rungs of the social hierarchy have been associated with a loosening
of the earlier administrative protocols and a steady erosion of the
institutional insulation of the decision-making process in public
administration and economic management. It is now common
practice for a low-caste chief minister in a State to proceed,
immediately upon assuming office, to transfer civil servants
belonging to upper castes and get pliant bureaucrats from his or
her own caste. Many members of the supposedly independent civil
service now try to curry favour with politicians to avoid transfers
to undesirable jobs and locations. Administrative appointments
outside the main civil service, like those to the boards of public
sector corporations, particularly those under State governments,
are often used as political sinecures to keep the clamouring
factions happy. What all this does to the institutional independence
of economic decision-taking bodies or the credibility of commit-
ment to long-run developmental policies is anybody's guess.

There is a certain nonchalance in the rampant corruption
among politicians in the newly emergent groups. Lower caste
leaders, when they come to power, are sometimes quite unapolo-
getic about being corrupt. They say that the upper castes in control
of the state have been corrupt for decades, and now it is their
turn.[15] Corruption is thus seen as a collective entitlement in an
amoral game of group equity.

No major political party in India is opposed to the strong
movements demanding large caste quotas in public sector jobs
and higher education for backward castes, in addition to those
stipulated in the Constitution for scheduled castes and tribes. As
the expansion of the public sector over the years created more
opportunities for secure jobs and, not infrequently, for the
associated extra, illicit income if the job was regulatory in nature,

[15] For a similar observation see Visvanathan (1997).

more and more mobilized groups in the democratic process have started using their low-caste status for staking a claim to the loot.

All this points to a major disjuncture between politics and economics in India so far as market reform is concerned. On the one hand, we are told that in recent years the era of market reform has arrived in India, and that there is a measure of political consensus that it is inexorable and irreversible. On the other hand, some of the major political events in the last decade or so that have captured public imagination constitute a phenomenon that is essentially anti-market: the propagation of group equity and caste rights, the carving of markets for new jobs in the public sector in protected niches, special dispensations and patronage for newly emergent groups, rampant caste-based violations of the institutional insulation of economic governance—all amounting to a drowning of considerations of efficiency in the name of inter-group equity.[16]

Cynics may even argue that the retreat of the State, implied by economic reform is now more acceptable to the upper classes

[16] It is arguable that inter-group equity may sometimes serve the cause of dynamic efficiency. To the extent special preferential policies for groups are supposed to cope with a historical handicap, their economic rationale may be akin to that behind the age-old argument for infant-industry protection in early stages of industrialization. Some disadvantaged groups may need temporary protection against competition so that they can participate in learning by doing and on-the-job skill formation before catching up with the others. Some of the standard arguments against infant-industry protection are then equally applicable to job reservation policies. For example, the 'infant', once protected, sometimes refuses to grow up; reservations, once adopted, are extremely difficult to reverse. Another argument against infant-industry protection is that even when the goal is justifiable, it may be achieved more efficiently through other policies. For example, a disadvantaged group may be helped by preferential loans, scholarships, job training programmes and extension services for its members, instead of job quotas that bar qualified candidates coming from advanced groups (in other words, equality of opportunity may be more justifable that insistence on equality of outcome). Such indirect policies of helping out backward groups are also less likely to generate political resentment (particularly because in this case the burden may be shared more evenly, whereas in the case of job quotas the redistributive burden falls on a small subset of the people in advanced communities).

and castes, not only because the regulatory and interventionist State has become too burdensome for the Indian economy, but also because these classes and castes are now losing their control over state power in the face of the emerging hordes of lower castes, and thus opting for greener pastures in the private sector (and abroad). This is a rather extreme, though interesting, hypothesis. It is certainly consistent with the fact that very few substantive reforms have yet been attempted in the agricultural sector[17]— a sector where appropriate reforms would have benefited the backward and lowly castes in massive . numbers.[18] It is also consistent with the fact that public enthusiasm for reforms is largely confined to the upper classes and the English media—say, the top decile or so in the income structure, which for some reason

[17] The major reason for this is, however, the inflation-sensitivity of the Indian polity. Substantial agricultural reforms will involve removal of controls on trade, which is likely to raise the price of major foodgrains that domestic consumers pay and the price of some raw materials (like cotton). Politicians of all parties are worried about the immediate consequences of such price rises, whatever their long-run benefits for producers may be. Indian farm lobbies (with the exception of some sections, e.g. those under leaders like Bhupinder Singh Mann or Sharad Joshi) are also not yet very active in demanding such reforms; they may be worried about the dismantling of the existing structure of food, fertilizer, water and electricity subsidies in exchange of receiving international agricultural prices may be too complex and politically risky a deal. In any case, since 1991, the 'disprotection' of the agricultural sector, in terms of relative inter-sectoral prices, has gone down considerably.

[18] The question has also been raised why, as the backward and lower castes are coming to acquire more political power, one does not see major reallocation of public expenditure on projects like health, education, housing, drinking water, and other development projects from which they would gain the most. Instead their leaders are often preoccupied with symbolic victories—like littering the countryside with Ambedkar statues, or, as anecdotes have it, keeping upper caste officers standing while the low-caste chief minister remains seated in the only chair kept in the office. To this one may respond and say that this probably is just a matter of time. These social and political changes have come to north India rather late; in south India, where such changes have taken place several decades back, it may not be a coincidence that there has been a lot more effective performance in the matter of social expenditure. This reflects the fact that in south India there has been a long history of social movement against exclusion of the lower castes from the public sphere, against their educational deprivation, etc. in a way more sustained

135

is called the 'middle class' in India—and even the most avid reformist politicians find it necessary to tone down their reform rhetoric at election time, when they have to face the unwashed masses.

There may be larger political–philosophical issues involved here. Many economists assume that market liberalism and competition is the natural order of things, and its unfolding in India has been blocked all these years only by our intellectual elites' socialist infatuation. It is not usually appreciated that Indian political culture may have a dominant anti-market streak that will not easily disappear, even if that supposedly imported infatuation fades away. Our collective passion for group equity, for group rather than individual rights, and the deep suspicion of competition in which the larger economic interests are given an opportunity to gobble up the small, work against the forces of market and allocational efficiency. This is not surprising in a country where the self-assertion of newly mobilized groups in an extremely hierarchical society takes the form of long-suppressed, group-specific expression and of clamouring for protected group-niches, where small people (small and middle peasants, self-employed artisans and shopkeepers, bazaar merchants and petty middlemen, clerks, school teachers and service workers) constitute an overwhelming majority of the population and their ranks are swelled by the inexorable demographic pressure and by the traditional inheritance practices involving subdivision of property. Gandhiji had given sensitive and eloquent expression to this anti-market, anti-big capital, small-is-beautiful populism and

---

and broad-based than in north India. One should also not lose sight of the fact that the upper caste opposition to social transformation is somewhat stronger in north India, as demographically upper castes constitute a much larger percentage of the population (for example, in U.P. and Bihar) than has been the case in most parts of south India. So new political victories of lower castes in north India get celebrated in the form of defiant symbols of social redemption and recognition aimed at solidifying the victories, rather than in committed attempts at changing the economic structure of deprivation.

136

mobilized it in the freedom movement against the British. Some other strands that grew out of our freedom movement, whether it is the ideas of Savarkar on the right (emphasizing community pride) or, on the left, those of Lohia (stressing lower-caste self-assertion against the westernized upper castes) or of Communists focusing on class mobilization—none of these ideas are overly concerned with individual rights[19]—also put a premium on group equity and dignity rather than individualist liberalism in the public sphere (even though the Indian vision of spirituality is often deeply individualistic). In recent decades those bearing the legacy of the Gandhian moral critique of market expansion and competition have joined forces with those espousing the left critique of capitalist exploitation of workers, peasants, and other small people and their rights over resources, in building active grassroots movements all over the country for the protection of the environment, of women's rights, and of the traditional livelihood of the indigenous people. In this growing movement 'development' or 'market' has almost become a dirty word, synonymous with dispossession of the little people and with despoliation of the environment. Major strands in the Indian political culture thus provide a none-too-hospitable climate for market reforms, and, contrary to the wishful thinking of many economists and journalists of the Indian 'pink press', the process of economic reforms is not likely to be smooth sailing for quite some time to come. The prospects for more reforms are not bleak, but one should not underestimate the scale and nature of opposition.

February 1998

[19] The leader who carried in him the tension between individual and group rights was B. R. Ambedkar, a constitutional lawyer who was also a major spokesman of an oppressed group.

References

de Tocqueville, A. (1835), *Democracy in America*, Vintage Books, New York, 1954.

Jenkins, R.S. (1997), *Democratic Adjustment: Explaining the Political Sustainability of Economic Reform in India*, D. Phil. Thesis, University of Sussex.

Nagaraj, R. (1997), 'What Has Happened since 1991? Assessment of India's Economic Reforms', *Economic and Political Weekly*, 18 November.

Srivastava, D.K. and T. K. Sen, (1997) *Government Subsidies in India*, National Institute of Public Finance and Policy, New Delhi.

Tendulkar, S.D., K. Sundaram, and L.R. Jain, (1996), *Macroeconomic Policies and Poverty in India: 1966–67 to 1993–94*, Report submitted to the South Asia Multidisciplinary Advisory Team, International Labour Organization, New Delhi.

Visvanathan, S. (1997), 'Gujaral's Red Fort Doctrine', *Economic and Political Weekly*, 20 September.

Appendix
Tables
(1980–81 to 1995–96)

TABLE I   TREND GROWTH RATES IN GDP
(per cent per year)

Years	Primary sector	Secondary sector	Tertiary sector	Total GDP
1980–81 to 1990–91	3.5	7.0	6.7	5.6
1980–81 to 1995–96	3.3	6.5	6.6	5.4

Source: Nagaraj (1997) on the basis of National Accounts Statistics.

TABLE II   MANUFACTURING SECTOR GROWTH 1981–96
(per cent per year)

Average of Years	Registered Manufacturing	Unregistered Manufacturing	Total Manufacturing
1981–85	7.7	4.1	6.2
1986–91	7.5	7.6	7.5
1992–96	7.1	5.7	6.6
1981–96	7.5	5.9	6.8

Source: Nagaraj (1997) on the basis of National Accounts Statistics.

141

TABLE III   STATEWISE PERCENTAGE OF PEOPLE BELOW OFFICIAL ALL-INDIA POVERTY LINES

State	Sector	1972–73	1977–78	1983	1987–88	1993–94
Andhra Pradesh	Rural	56.7	42.7	34.9	31.6	28.6
	Urban	51.1	41.9	35.5	40.0	36.4
Assam	Rural	59.7	62.5	49.2	53.1	58.4
	Urban	31.6	33.7	21.0	11.4	10.2
Bihar	Rural	68.1	67.7	70.4	66.3	65.5
	Urban	53.1	51.9	51.3	56.7	45.9
Gujarat	Rural	53.3	43.7	36.3	41.6	30.1
	Urban	57.3	40.7	37.3	38.8	29.2
Haryana	Rural	25.4	32.1	24.0	23.2	30.1
	Urban	32.7	36.9	21.3	18.3	11.2
Karnataka	Rsural	49.4	49.7	40.2	42.3	38.1
	Urban	53.8	48.9	37.7	45.0	33.4
Kerala	Rural	67.4	57.6	47.2	44.0	34.8
	Urban	61.9	58.2	47.8	44.5	29.2
Madhya Pradesh	Rural	63.6	64.3	54.0	49.8	36.7
	Urban	60.9	61.3	52.0	46.0	46.7

(Cont.)

Maharashtra	Rural	66.6	68.3	54.0	54.2	51.0
	Urban	42.6	39.2	40.4	35.6	33.7
Orissa	Rural	73.0	71.9	65.0	65.6	59.5
	Urban	54.0	54.2	52.5	44.5	38.9
Punjab	Rural	25.0	20.4	18.4	21.0	16.7
	Urban	22.0	26.6	21.6	11.2	7.0
Rajasthan	Rural	50.5	40.5	42.0	41.9	26.4
	Urban	51.6	44.1	37.2	41.5	31.8
Tamil Nadu	Rural	59.0	59.5	56.8	51.3	37.9
	Urban	52.8	49.4	45.1	39.2	38.5
Uttar Pradesh	Rural	51.2	50.7	49.8	47.7	39.2
	Urban	56.2	54.2	48.1	41.9	35.2
West Bengal	Rural	74.6	72.4	65.9	57.2	53.3
	Urban	37.3	34.8	28.8	30.6	20.8
All-India	Rural	57.2	54.5	49.0	44.9	39.7
	Urban	47.0	43.0	38.3	36.5	30.9

Source: Tendulkar, Sundaram, and Jain (1996). These estimates are based on per capita expenditure distribution data collected by the National Sample Survey, the Planning Commission all-India poverty line of monthly per capita expenditure of Rs 49.09 (rural) and Rs 56.64 (urban) at 1973–74 prices, and the State-specific poverty lines adjusted for State-specific prices.

TABLE IV   STATE-WISE COMPOSITE INDEX OF DEPRIVATION BASED ON CHILDREN'S STUNTING, BIRTH CONDITION AND FEMALE ILLITERACY IN RURAL AREAS IN 1994

State	*Average percentage of the relevant population thus deprived*
Andhra Pradesh	41.6
Bihar	65.6
Gujarat	45.2
Haryana	46.8
Himachal Pradesh	48.4
Karnataka	47.5
Kerala	12.0
Madhya Pradesh	56.3
Maharashtra	46.3
Northeastern regions (taken together)	40.4
Orissa	55.1
Punjab	35.5
Rajasthan	65.8
Tamil Nadu	29.6
Uttar Pradesh	60.6
West Bengal	53.2
Rural India	52.3

Source: National Council of Applied Economic Research sample survey estimates, based on what the UNDP's *Human Development Report 1996* calls 'capability poverty measure', averaging indicators for (a) the percentage of children 0–4 years who are underweight ('stunted', i.e. 3 standard deviations below median), (b) the percentage of births unattended by trained health personnel, and (c) the percentage of women aged fifteen years and above who are illiterate.

TABLE V   UNEMPLOYMENT RATES FOR MEN AND WOMEN
IN LABOUR FORCE (Per cent)

Years	Sector	Male	Female	Total
1983	Rural	7.5	9.0	7.9
	Urban	9.2	11.0	9.5
	All-India	7.9	9.2	8.2
1987–88	Rural	4.6	6.9	5.2
	Urban	8.8	12.0	9.3
	All-India	5.5	7.6	6.0
1993–94	Rural	5.6	5.6	5.6
	Urban	6.7	10.5	7.4
	All-India	5.9	6.3	6.0

Source: National Sample Survey daily-status unemployment data, where the unemployment rate is defined as the number of days seeking (or being available for) work in the reference week as percentage of total number of days in the labour force in that period.

TABLE VI   DISTRIBUTION OF CULTIVATED LAND

Size Class	Year	Percentage of Holidings	Percentage of Area Operated
Marginal	1960–61	40.7	6.7
(less than 1	1970–71	50.6	9.0
hectare)	1980–81	56.7	12.0
	1990–91	59.0	14.9
Small	1960–61	22.3	12.2
(1–2 hectares)	1970–71	19.1	11.9
	1980–81	18.1	14.1
	1990–91	19.0	17.3
Semi-Medium	1960–61	18.9	20.0
(2–4 hectares)	1970–71	15.2	18.5
	1980–81	14.0	21.2
	1990–91	13.2	23.2

(Cont.)

Size Class	Year	Percentage of Holidings	Percentage of Area Operated
Medium	1960–61	13.4	30.4
(4–10 hectares)	1970–71	11.2	29.7
	1980–81	9.1	29.0
	1990–91	7.2	27.2
Large	1960–61	4.7	30.7
(10 hectares	1970–71	3.9	30.9
and above)	1980–81	2.4	23.0
	1990–91	1.6	17.4

Source: Agricultural Census.

TABLE VII   STATE-WISE INFRASTRUCTURAL DEVELOPMENT INDEX (relative to All-India Average)

State	1980–81	1993–94
Andhra Pradesh	98.1	96.1
Assam	77.7	78.9
Bihar	83.5	81.1
Gujarat	123.0	122.4
Haryana	145.5	141.3
Himachal Pradesh	83.5	98.8
Jammu and Kashmir	88.7	84.0
Karnataka	94.8	96.9
Kerala	158.1	157.1
Madhya Pradesh	62.1	75.3
Maharashtra	120.1	107.0
Orissa	81.5	97.0
Punjab	207.3	191.4
Rajasthan	74.4	83.0
Tamil Nadu	158.6	144.0
Uttar Pradesh	97.7	103.3
West Bengal	110.6	94.2
All-India	100.0	100.0

Source: Estimates by the Centre for Monitoring the Indian Economy.

TABLE VIII   DISTRIBUTION OF ASSETS IN THE CORPORATE SECTOR BY OWNERSHIP (in per cent)

Ownership Group	1990	1996
Government	64.1	60.4
Indian Private Sector	31.5	35.6
Top 50 Indian Business Houses	18.0	15.7
Foreign Private Sector	4.4	3.9
Private Sector	35.9	39.6
Total	100.0	100.0

Source: Center for Monitoring the Indian Economy, on the basis of a sample survey.

TABLE IX   GOVERNMENT SUBSIDIES (BUDGET-BASED) IN 1994–95 (in Rs billion)

	Centre	State	All-India
1. Subsidies to Merit Goods or Services	55.22 (16.9)	271.07 (83.1)	326.29 (100.0)
2. Subsidies to Non-Merit Goods or Services	375.67 (36.1)	666.48 (63.9)	1042.15 (100.0)
3. Surplus Sectors (Merit and Non-Merit)	−46.43 (49.1)	−48.19 (50.9)	−92.62 (100.0)
4. Total Subsidies Net of Surplus (1+2+3)	384.46 (30.2)	889.36 (69.8)	1273.82 (100.0)

Source: Srivastava and Sen (1997). The figures in parenthesis refer to percentage of all-India figures. Merit goods and services include elementary education, public health, sewerage and sanitation, many social welfare schemes, soil and water conservation, environmental forestry and wildlife, agricultural research, flood control and drainage, roads and bridges, and various scientific research. Expenditure on public goods like defence and general administration has been excluded out of the ambit of the subsidies computed above. Surplus sectors refer to those sectors where a surplus (negative subsidy) is generated.

TABLE X INTERNAL DEBT OF CENTRAL AND STATE GOVERNMENTS IN 1996–97 (in Rs billion)

State	Total Internal Debt
Andhra Pradesh	174.7
Arunachal Pradesh	6.3
Assam	56.0
Bihar	187.0
Delhi	20.8
Goa	12.7
Gujarat	126.8
Haryana	68.6
Himachal Pradesh	29.6
Jammu and Kashmir	48.9
Karnataka	113.2
Kerala	117.9
Madhya Pradesh	139.2
Maharashtra	211.9
Manipur	6.4
Meghalaya	5.4
Mizoram	4.9
Nagaland	10.3
Orissa	107.7
Punjab	155.3
Rajasthan	140.2
Sikkim	3.2
Tamil Nadu	146.5
Tripura	10.0
Uttar Pradesh	348.9
West Bengal	186.2
All States taken together	2439.2
Central Government	3349.0
GDP (at current market prices)	12600.0

Name Index

de Tocqueville, A. 132

Jenkins, R. S. 120, 125, 126

Nagraj, R. 121, 123 n.4

Srivasteva, D. K. and T. K. Sen
127–8

Visvanathan, S. 133 n.5

Subject Index

Subject Index

Fifth Pay Commission Report 123
  revision of pay in 129
financial sector reforms 127

Gandhian critique of market
  expansion 136–7
growth rate 122, GDP 141
  time series data on 121
group(s), dominant interest 131
  equity 136
  historically subordinate 132

income, illicit 126
India, economic policy change 119
  federal transfers in 130
  regulatory State in 131–2
  political equilibrium in 130–31
Industrial Disputes Act 125
inflation and Indian State 128 n.11,
  135 n.17
infrastructure as bottleneck 122
  development, inter-state index
    146
insurance sector 120, 127
interest rate structure 124
  deregulation 127 n.8
investment, foreign 124 n.6
  private 130

labour, laws reform 126
land, distribution of cultivated
  145–6
  political manipulation of 126
liberalization, effect on growth of
  121
  political support for 124

macroeconomic stabilization 122
  credit crunch 124
manufacturing sector 121
  growth 141

unregistered 122
mobilization, class 137
  group 136
  resource 130

National Institute of Public Finance
  and Policy 127

organized labour 123

Planning Commission, development
  grants 129
politics, coalition 120
  disjunctive in economics and
    134
political, culture and market reform
  134, 136, 137
  equilibrium and lower castes
    132–3
politicians, corruption and 133
poverty line, people below 142–3
  capability poverty measure 144
prices 135
primary sector 121
privatization 123
public enterprises, monopoly and
  126
  total factor productivity of 123
public sector, banks 127
  fiscal deficit in 128

reform, coalitions and 120, 132
  lack of opposition to 124–6
  pace/prospect of 119
  political economy of 119, 123
  States and 130
  market 134
regional, fragmentation of power
  125, 130
  government 131
  resistance to reform 127